4.98

A Korean
Minjung Theology
— an old testament perspective

Cyris H.S. Moon

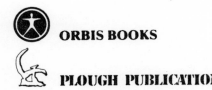

ORBIS BOOKS

PLOUGH PUBLICATIONS

Copyright ⓒ 1985 Plough Publications

Published by: Orbis Books, Maryknoll NY 10545
Plough Publications, 48 Princess Margaret Rd.,
Kowloon, Hong Kong

Manufactured in Hong Kong

Orbis/ISBN   0-88344-250-7
Plough/ISBN   962-7043-10-9

Cover Design: Angela Kang

Contents

Contents

Preface

Christian theology has been a discipline primarily defined in the historical context, thought, and culture of Europe and America. For many years non-Westerners have been taught and expected to theologize and express Christianity in Western garb. Thus, the situation of the people of the Third World has often been overlooked, as their socio-economic-political needs have been ignored in past theological discussions. Recently, however, there seems to be a renaissance of theologizing in the Third World countries.

If we understand that theology emerges as a human reflection of God's activity in the history and life of a particular people in a particular time and context, it is not surprising to see in the Third World today, and especially in Korea, an awareness and need to identify indigenous cultural heritages. The assertion being made today in Korea is that God speaks to every race and culture, and that the message communicated is adapted according to the mode of the hearer in each particular historical context.

Koreans today are making great efforts to recover their own culture and to reappropriate it to form the basis of the *minjung's* (people's) identity and theology. It is also being asserted that the axis of Christianity is moving from the West to the East with an average of one million converts being added yearly to the Christian community in the East. By the year 2000 it is predicted that about 80 percent of the population of Korea will be Christians. This implies that Korea, with its non-Western cultural environment, is bound to leave its imprint on the expression of Christian faith and life in the future.

It is said that the Korean people do not want any longer to be the objects of the historical process of theologizing but rather to be its subjects and to play a definitive role in Korean history today. The kingdom of God is here. The subject of the kingdom is the whole human race, including Koreans. The Korean church is conscious of its history. These perceptions seem to be those held by many of the contributors of articles published in the book *Minjung Theology* (CCA, Singapore, 1982; Zed Press, London, 1984; and Orbis Books, Maryknoll, N.Y., 1984).

At this point, it should be stated that I make no claim that my book is steeped with original theological thought. Nor is it my intention to duplicate the above-mentioned book. Those who would like to know more about *minjung* theology from the standpoint of the many theologians in Korea who initially formulated *minjung* theology should read that book first.

Instead, a sociological method of biblical interpretation is proposed in my book. We Koreans believe that our experiences match in many ways the context of the biblical world. By reading the Bible from a sociological point of view, the Old Testament (as well as the New) is seen to show Yahweh as on the side of the poor and the oppressed. The struggle for liberation in Korea that is taking place in the work of the Urban Industrial Missions, in the student activities of the World Student Christian Federation of Korea, and furthermore in the lives of the oppressed people in the streets of Korea — that is where theological action is. We are called to read the Bible in a way that liberates it from our blindness to the relativity of our own point of view. It appears that the social matrix from which biblical inter-pretation is made must be extended to the social matrix of the inter-preter to bridge the gap between religion and the rest of life.

It is my hope that this book will stimulate readers to raise new questions. The liberating work of Yahweh is provocative and unsettling. Those who follow Jesus Christ are compelled to ask again and again whether they rightly understand what it means to be liberated with Yahweh's freedom.

I am grateful to many people for their assistance in the pre-paration of this small book : Mr. Ahn Jaewoon, the General Secretary of the Asian/Pacific region of the World Student Christian Federation, encouraged me to write this book. During a seminar, the Advanced Pastoral Studies students at San Francisco Theological Seminary in the summers of 1982 and 1983 contributed much in the discussion of *minjung* theology from the Old Testament perspective. The editorial members of Plough Publications offered me many valuable suggestions for improvement. Jeff Jordan and Fred Broadwell worked with me on the final touches of this book. My three daughters, Rachel Young-jin, Esther Young-me, and Hannah Young-sil, typed the manuscript. Last but not least, I want to record many thanks to my helpful and loving wife who has strengthened me by her faithfulness and love.

December 1984
Moon, Hee-suk Cyris
Seoul, Korea

Introduction

For some time, many theologians in Korea have been discussing numerous issues such as the question of indigenized, contextual, secular, and political theology. In the early years of the 1970s a new discussion centered on the *minjung* in Korea. The theologians were concerned with the theme of *minjung* liberation. It was at this time that many theologians were dismissed from their posts in seminaries and universities because of their position of defending the oppressed and students imprisoned by the Korean Central Intelligence agents implementing the oppressive policies of the Park Chung Hee regime. Some of the dismissed theologians and many other theologians who were still able to teach under government surveillance began to experience the sufferings of the *minjung*. Thus, they were willing to learn and reflect theologically upon the *minjung's* life in Korea. They began to write, sometimes while in prison, on the theme of the liberation of these *minjung*. Along with the theologians, there were nontheologians, such as poets and other intellectual people, who also were having the same kind of experiences as the theologians. Therefore, not all the articles being written at that time about the *minjung* were theological. "Quite a few were historical inquires, and others were sociological studies. There were also studies of *minjung* literature, drama, and art. Consequently, there were lively interactions between theological reflections on the *minjung* and secular intellectual efforts to articulate the reality of the *minjung*."[1]

In order to formulate *minjung* theology, theologians, first of all, have tried to clarify the *minjung* in Korean historical terms. In those attempts the social biography of the *minjung* has been an important point of reference. In other words, the social history of the *minjung* liberation movements (such as the *Tonghak* Movement, 1895, the March First Independence Movement, 1919, and the April 19th Student Revolt, 1960), the *minjung* religious traditions, and the past and the present cultural expressions of the *minjung* are all being studied.[2]

The other very significant reference points for *minjung* theology are the Bible and Christian theology. *Minjung* theologians are keen to discover the socio-economic-political background of the Old and the New Testaments so these may be studied from the *minjung's* perspective. Of paricular interest in the area of the Old Testament are the Hebrews (who can be equated with the people called *habiru*), the reign of Solomon, who advocated the so-called "Royal Consciousness",[3] and the prophetic traditions. As for the area of theology, special attention is being given to studies on theodicy, apocalyptic, the suffering servant, and the messianic spirit (Holy Spirit).[4]

The essential concern of the *minjung* theologians using these two reference points is to interweave the Korean *minjung's* story and the Old Testament story. That is what I have attempted to do in this book: that is, study the history of Korean *minjung* as reflected in the Old Testament stories. In so doing, I am trying to accomplish several things. First of all, I wish to review the background of the Korean *minjung* using the Old Testament as a historical basis. The similarities between biblical history and Korean history are clearly made evident. Second, I hope to clarify the position of today's *minjung* by using the insight that the Old Testament history provides. And finally, with this new perspective in mind, I outline the task that lies ahead for both the *minjung* and their supporters. I firmly believe that this study is both relevant and crucial in today's struggle for *minjung* liberation.

1.

An Introduction

to the *Minjung*

Today in Korean society the word *minjung* is being looked at with both interest and concern. Talk of the *minjung's* conscientization, the *minjung* as the subjects of history, and *minjung* theology has become increasingly common. Furthermore, the term is now used not only by the *minjung* themselves, but also by the people who wish to identify with the sufferings of the *minjung*. Thus it has become an expression of consciousness. Yet what do we mean when we say "the *minjung*"?

First of all, let us begin with a definition of the word. *Minjung* (民衆) is a Korean word composed of two Chinese character: *min*, which means "people," and *jung* which means "the mass." Literally, then, this would be translated into English as "the mass of people." However this simple translation does not fully reflect what is meant by the term, for *minjung* is not a concept or object which can be easily explained or defined. Rather, *minjung* expresses a living reality which is dynamic, changing, and complex. [1] This living reality defines its own existence through its actions and the place it makes for itself in history, making it difficult to come to any agreement regarding the precise definition of the term. But as a starting point I would like to posit the following general definition of *minjung*: "The *minjung* are those who are oppressed politically, exploited economically, alienated socially, and kept uneducated in cultural and intellectual matters." [2]

Another way of expressing this would be to say that the *minjung* are *han*-ridden people. *Han* (恨) is also a Korean word, which might be translated as "grudge" or "resentment." *Han* is the anger and resentment of the *minjung* which has been turned inward and intensified as they become the objects of injustice upon injustice. It is the result of being repressed for an extended period of time by external forces: political oppression, economic exploitation, social alienation, and restrictions against becoming educated in cultural and intellectual matters.

Han is a hallmark of the Korean *minjung*. They have a troubled social biography which stretches back for centuries; they have suffered repeated foreign invasions and internal exploitation. For thirty-six years they endured humiliation under Japanese colonial rule. National emancipation in 1945 did not improve the situation at all, for the nation was divided into two hostile parts by the two superpowers for their own selfish interests. The tragedies brought about by the national division are beyond description. [3]

Herein lies the complex nature of the *han* of the Korean *minjung*. As a people of a small and weak nation, they hate and resent the wrongs done to them by the surrounding nations whose might they cannot overcome. Yet although they do not know how their hopes might be actualized, being pressed by ever-increasing hopes for a free and just world, they cannot give up their yearning for a new future. Thus they are torn between hope and hopelessness.

Han, however, is a starting point for a new human history. Through the experience of *han* one's spiritual eyes are opened and one is enabled to see the deep truths about life. In *han*, we come to see the infinite value of personhood and are able to assert our precious rights as human beings. In *han* we see clearly what is good and evil and learn to hate evil and love good. In *han* we encounter God who comes down to the *han*-ridden people and justifies their plight. With *han* as our point of departure we begin to dream of a new, alternative future and to dedicate ourselves to the cause of making that future a reality. [4]

Thus, the word *minjung* must be differentiated from the term *paeksung* (百性), which denotes the common people who *accept* oppression and enslavement. The meaning of *minjung* is also different from that of the term *inmin* (人民), which is used in China to denote the national entity.

2.

The Hebrews

and the Exodus

At the outset, we should note that the Old Testament is a collection of writings by scribes, priests, and other learned people from a society dominated by a patriarchy. The *minjung* of the Old Testament did not participate in writing these documents. Therefore, these writings portray the world from the perspective of men and royalty. From the vantage point of the rulers they describe events and activities engaged in primarily by men (such as war, cult, and government). However, the Old Testament is also filled with stories of liberation. So although the *minjung* of the Old Testament could not and did not write their own aspirations and biographies of suffering and oppression, there is ample evidence of the liberation movement of the *minjung* in the Old Testament.

The first such movement that comes instantly to mind is that of the Exodus, which took place in the thirteenth century B.C. The Hebrews, during the reign of Ramses II, [1] were being forced to serve as slaves under the repressive rule of the Egyptians. Moses emerged as the liberator of the Hebrews and brought about the confrontation between himself and the Pharaoh that eventually led to the Hebrews' liberation. In order to appreciate the enormousness of this achievement, we must first focus our attention on the object of Moses' concern: the Hebrew slaves, the despised, the powerless, the outcasts, and those who had no rights at all. Indeed, Moses' greatness lies in his identifying himself with these people in order to liberate them.

The word *habiru* (which is often equated with the word "Hebrew" and is also spelled *apiru or habiru*) is a term that can be traced to records in the second millennium B.C. in Egypt, Babylonia, Syria, and Palestine; it appears frequently also in the oldest extant tablets and written records. The nature and identity of the *habiru* have been the subject of considerable literature, for the term provides a clue to who the *minjung* of that time were. The 1976 supplementary volume of *The Interpreter's Dictionary of the Bible* describes the *habiru* as mercenary soldiers, people under treaty, and prisoners of war. [2] Other sources suggest that they were outlaws, outcasts, and those who stood outside the dominant social system. At any rate, they most certainly were rebels standing in defiance of the prevailing social or power structure.[3] The *habiru*, therefore, were part of the *minjung* of their time, driven by their *han* (grudge or resentment)[4] to act against what they felt to be injustices imposed on them by those in power.

The social system in Egypt was a strict bureaucracy within which the functions of the various classes were strictly regulated. The structure of the state was largely dependent on four influential factors: the king, his civil servants, the army, and the priests. These were the dominating groups which exerted their power over everyone else, particularly the Hebrews.

Apart from the individuals who were closely connected with some of the basic institutions of the country, there were two more groups of people. The first group consisted of the free citizens, that is, the peasants and tillers of the land. These individuals, though free in the technical sense of the word, were actually bound to the soil they worked, often living on a starvation level. And then, apart from the free population, there was a large group of slaves spread throughout the land.

There were three types of slaves: those who worked as the personal property of individuals, those who worked as state-owned property on public works or military projects, and those who were temple slaves. How they were treated varied according to times and circumstances, but if the members of the lower class of free citizens were referred to as "children of nobodies," one can well imagine in what regard a slave was held. In short, the slaves were the lowest class of people, and under the oppressive Egyptian system, they suffered total and brutal exploitation.

Despite the fact that the Hebrews suffered this complete loss of their rights and freedom, Moses had difficulty in persuading them to act toward achieving their liberty. According to Exodus 3:1-14, he had to make them realize that they had to escape from Egypt in order to be a liberated people. This is important, for one would think that because the Hebrews had suffered an oppressed life, they would realize that the only way to liberation was to trust God and Moses and act accordingly. However, it seems that they did not have this kind of trust. As a result of such a long and cruel oppression by the Egyptians, the Hebrews had developed the mentality of slaves. This is one way rulers can prevent rebellion before it begins: they break the spirit of their slaves by driving them more severely and depriving them of tolerable living conditions. As the people are deprived of their humanity, they are subordinated. It is not difficult to see why a completely dominated people, who are reduced to being concerned only with eating the food distributed regularly by the ruler, would not want to risk escape from the protection of the ruler and make a long journey to a virtual wasteland.

In this way, the Exodus narrative points out an important fact: Yahweh cannot be the sole actor in the movement for liberation. Rather, humanity is invited to act as a partner with God. People are to assist in the restoration of their own rights which have been infringed upon, a concept which differs from the idea that the fulfillment of all human history is carried out under God's sovereignty alone. The writers of Exodus stress that if oppressed people are to obtain liberation, they must—with God's aid—confront the pharaohs of the world: in order for the Hebrews to participate in the struggle for their human rights, they had first to realize that it was Pharaoh who had infringed upon their rights and that their struggle had to begin with a direct confrontation with Pharaoh. Thus, the third chapter of Exodus says that Moses was ordered to confront Pharaoh in order to help the Hebrews escape from slavery.

At the same time, the writers of Exodus did not presume to say that the Hebrews deserved to receive God's protection and the restoration of their human rights. Rather, their liberation was the result of God's gracious action. Thus Exodus reveals what anyone who participates in the struggle for liberation comes eventually to realize: God is on the side of the oppressed and downtrodden and will always give encouragement and protection to them. In fact, some of the first words with which God is introduced to Moses in the Exodus narrative indicate that God is concerned with the *minjung*. In Exodus 3:7 God states: "I have seen indeed the affliction of my people which are in Egypt." God relates not just in a general way as the creator of human beings, but as concerned with a specific oppressed people to whom Moses stands in a special relationship.

In the Hebrew text of Exodus 3:7 the verbal construction of the form "I have seen" makes the "seeing" an emphatic process. Furthermore, the little phrase "which are in Egypt," instead of the simpler "in Egypt," seems to show an incongruent situation: God's *minjung* are in Egypt when they should be in the promised land. At this point it should be remembered that the Hebrews must have regarded the promised land as a kind of never-never land, and to the question "Whose people are you?" they would very likely have answered: "Do you not see that we are Pharaoh's people?" Thus, it is significant that even while the people did not call themselves Yahweh's people, Yahweh immediately thinks of them as "my people." In other words, God owns them long before they own God.

Moreover, when in Exodus 3:6 the encounter between God and Moses is linked to the patriarchs, the faithfulness and reliability of God are emphasized. God is not one to change God's mind or to forget; God stands true to God's promise. In Exodus 3 God is revealed as a liberator first, as one who would liberate God's minjung from bondage and settle them in a land of their own. This liberation is also connected with a religious purpose which is clearly stated in Exodus 3:12: "God said, 'But I will be with you; and this shall be the sign for you, that I have sent you; when you have brought forth the people out of Egypt, you shall serve God upon this mountain.' "

Apart from the revelation of God in this personal and historical sense we have at this encounter between God and Moses a further statement (Exod. 3:14) concerning God's personal self, a statement which stands unique even in the pages of the Old Testament. It furnishes us with the only explanation of the name Yahweh, a name which is used more than six thousand times in the Old Testament. When we consider the meaning of the name Yahweh as given to Moses in the striking phrase "I am who I am," two factors seem to emerge clearly. On the one hand, the words strike us as mysterious, enigmatic; they seem to conceal more than to reveal; on the other hand, considering ation in which they were spoken, they are meant to reassure, to al the presence of God.

"I am who I am" tells us indeed that we are face to face with a God whose being is beyond comprehension, beyond human intellect which would seek to define God within certain categories of thought. The essential Being of God cannot be understood by reference to human beings or nature, for God stands outside time and space and God's Being is beyond cause and effect. The infinite and eternal, that which transcends our realm altogether, is implied in the statement "I am who I am." Yet this Being of God is not expressed in a form which could make God synonymous with the idea of the infinite or eternal, for Being is linked here to the personal "I." God is not to be understood as an impersonal force behind the universe; rather God is revealed as a personal Being. As the eternal "I am" (the phrase could also be rendered "I shall be who I shall be"), God makes history indeed, for this transcendent God is revealed as being actively present within the realm of human experience. The phrase "I am who I am" stresses the truth of both the transcendence and the immanence of God. God's Being is not only "throned afar," but God is also the God of justice and compassion who is a very helpful presence in time of oppression and trouble. And it is obvious that the revelation of the name of God given to Moses has the purpose of assuring him and the Hebrews of the very real presence of God who will act justly for the liberation of the *minjung*. "I am who I am" should be understood in the sense of "you can take my presence as a guarantee for action on your behalf for the cause of justice and compassion." Thus, with the assurance of Yahweh, the Hebrews began to make their freedom march, crossing the Red Sea and the wilderness. And after many years of wandering, they finally found themselves in Canaan, the promised land.

As the contextual situation of this Exodus motif is reconstructed, parallels between it and Korea come to light. For instance, Koreans, like the Hebrews, suffered for years under the domination of ruthless governments and foreign oppressors. In order to see these parallels more clearly, let us now turn briefly to a short history of the Korean people.

According to tradition, Korean history dates back to 2333 B.C. when Tangun, the son of a bear, founded Korea. In early history it appears that tribal communities developed and matured into three states: Koguryo in the North; and Silla and Paekche in the South. It was during this era, the Three Kingdom Period (57 B.C.-A.D. 668), that Korean recorded history began. It was also during this period that Buddhism was first introduced into Korea by the Chinese.

By 668, with the help of the T'ang Dynasty in China, the state of Silla had unified Korea. However, in the latter part of the ninth century, the power of the Silla Dynasty began to weaken steadily. There were several reasons for this decline. The hereditary nature of the government positions had resulted in a ruling elite which was restricted to members from a few clans. These family factions were constantly vying for power and influence; this weakened the central government.

Out of all this political chaos a new leadership finally emerged. In 918 Wan Kon defeated his opponents and founded the Koryo Dynasty. He immediately instituted several new ordinances and changes. One such change was in the system of land ownership. It was declared that all property was to belong to the government, the high officials, and the Buddhist priesthood. During this period, Buddhism reached its height of power. This was due to the fact that the aristocracy supported Buddhism, as it promised happiness for the ruling class and Buddha's protection for the king. The priests gradually became powerful landowners, and their influence on political decisions greatly increased. Toward the end of the fourteenth century, Buddhist priests controlled much of the national economy and became de facto rulers in many areas.

From 1219 to 1392 the country was in deep trouble. In 1219, the new Mongolian leadership in China invaded Korea and Koryo became a tributary state. In the midst of this political turmoil, many of the ruling elite and Buddhist priesthood began to exercise their power ruthlessly. This led to excessive exploitation of the *minjung,* especially the peasantry, which in turn resulted in rebellion and unrest.

Because of these problems, the government desperately tried to institute several reform programs. These programs had a two-fold purpose: one, the revitalization of the nation after almost a century of Mongol domination and, two, the elimination of the social and political abuses of the *minjung* for which the Buddhist priesthood was held responsible. The persons initiating the reforms were the Confucian scholar-officials, those who had obtained their positions by passing the civil service examinations.

In 1392, Yi Songgye, the newly risen military leader, overthrew the Koryo Dynasty, thus founding the Yi Dynasty. Yi immediately turned the new administration over to the classical scholars, who then instituted numerous reform programs. All of the estates were confiscated and redistributed to those who had been loyal to Yi Songgye. In addition, Buddhism was deemed unacceptable as the official religion; Confucianism, or more accurately Neo-Confucianism, was substituted for it. There were several reasons for this change. Toward the end of the Koryo period there was a definite deterioration in the moral and spiritual leadership of the Buddhist priests. As they grew wealthier and more powerful, they also became more corrupt. Thus, in order for the new dynasty to retain its position and increase its power, it was imperative that the Buddhists lose their influence and power. The administration confiscated all temple property and forbade all Buddhist activities. Not surprisingly, this change received wide support. An anti-Buddhist movement had already started in the late Koryo years as a result of the resentment generated by the priests' manipulation of power and wealth. Thus the switch from Buddhism to Neo-Confucianism was, for most of the *minjung*, a welcome change. However, as it turned out, this shift to Neo-Confucianism was not beneficial to the *minjung,* for basically two social strata emerged. They were the *yang ban* (the ruling class people) and the *xiang rom* (the slaves, the landless peasants, the powerless, and the lower class people).

The Korean Confucian scholars believed that the universe was comprised of two forces which were manifested in light and darkness, heaven and earth, male and female. These forces were called *Yang* and *Yin.* According to the scholars, *Yang,* which symbolized heaven, was superior to *Yin,* symbolizing earth. As long as this natural hierarchy was obeyed, the human world and the cosmic order would be in balance, and society would be in harmony and peace. If this hierarchical system was disrupted, a state of barbarism and chaos in which human desires would be uncontrolled would result. Thus, according to the Confucianists, a harmonious and orderly society could exist only when the *minjung* had served their superiors, the *yang ban.* The Confucianists also taught that the female was created especially for the purposes of procreation and of giving pleasure to the male. Thus, they insisted upon the inferiority of women, placing them in the same class as slaves.[5] *Xiang rom* and women were the *minjung* of the time.

During the reign of King Sungjong (1469-1494), the classical scholars emerged as a new force, and the number of the ruling class increased. This was followed by the reign of King Kusanghaegun (1608-1623), during which many independent middle-class farmers and wholesale dealers also became part of the ruling class. Yet the two distinct classes remained evident until the end of the Yi Dynasty in 1910. In this kind of socio-economico-political context Protestant Christianity was introduced to Korea in the year 1884.

Dr. Horace N. Allen was the first Protestant missionary (co-worker) to come to Korea. A member of the Presbyterian Mission Board, he brought courage, vision, and devotion with him in his desire to be a partner with the Koreans to work for the extension of God's kingdom. However, one of the policies of the Yi Dynasty toward the West at that time was *choksa chongwi* ("expel the wrong and defend the right"). This policy was evident in a series of persecutions of the Catholics (who came to Korea in 1784) and in an uncompromising closed door policy toward the Western powers.[6] Therefore, Dr. Allen arrived in Korea through the "back door" of the American legation, which appointed him the legation doctor. With his Western medical skills he gradually gained the favor of the royal family and laid a foundation for future mission work. On April 5, 1885, Rev. M. G. Underwood, a Presbyterian missionary, and Henry Apenzeller, a Methodist missionary, and his wife joined Dr. Allen. As time passed, the missionary community grew and carried out a considerable amount of medical work. [7]

A landmark occasion for the American Protestant mission was the opening of a school for girls in 1885. The opportunities that the missionaries made available through education were both for girls (who were still considered to be inferior creatures) as well as boys of the *minjung*. The sons of the *yang ban* were not attracted to the schools. [8]

Meanwhile, because Christian evangelism was still banned, the work of the American mission had to be done among the *minjung*, and it had to be secret and underground work. The early missionaries tried to gain the favor of the government, being cautious and patient in doing their work to gain the confidence of the government and the people.

They were very busy, for, on the one hand, the missionaries were using the good offices of the American legation while, on the other hand, they were slowly penetrating the lower class, that is, the *minjung,* of the Korean society.[9]

During this period the missionaries made a major breakthrough. Discovering that *Hangul,* the Korean vernacular script, was being despised and neglected, they picked it to study and to use to communicate to the *minjung* of Korea. Thus the medium through which they worked was the language of the *minjung,* while Chinese was the official written language of the Korean officialdom and the *yang ban* class. Using this medium encouraged and facilitated the contact of the Christian message and of its missionary bearers with the *minjung* in Korea. This was the beginning of the process of rehabilitating the language of the Korean *minjung.*[10]

Next, the Bible was translated into *Hangul.* The translation of the New Testament began in 1887, and by 1900 the entire Bible was translated into the Korean vernacular. Other books and tracts were also published; the circulation of these and of the Bible became the most effective strategy of the missionaries in spreading the gospel of Jesus Christ.

In January 1893, the early Protestant missionaries adopted a very significant mission policy, which was called the "Nevius Method." The four articles of the policy were outlined as follows:

1. It is better to aim at the conversion of the working classes than that of the higher classes.
2. The conversion of women and the training of Christian girls should be a special aim, since mothers exercise so important an influence over future generations.
3. The Word of God converts where humankind is without resources; therefore it is most important that we make every effort to place a clear translation of the Bible before the people as soon as possible.
4. The mass of Koreans must be led to Christ by their own fellow country men; therefore we shall thoroughly train a few as evangelists rather than preach to a multitude ourselves. [11]

During the latter years of the Yi Dynasty there were also many important political events that took place. Much social unrest and many political revolts by the *minjung* against the ruling class occurred. Among them, one event deserves special attention. That is the *Tonghak* Rebellion. Among the *yang ban* class the buying and selling of government positions was a common practice. Then, anyone who purchased an official position could generally reimburse himself through extortion. Taxes and levies were increased by local and national governments until they reached three or four times the legal rate. Extravagance, licentiousness, and debauchery were the order of the day at the court. The suffering *minjung* could no longer remain silent. In 1895, the *Tonghaks,* a group mostly comprised of poor peasants, rose in rebellion in the South.[12] This *Tonghak* Rebellion had both religious and political significance. In many ways, it represented the first indigenous, organized *minjung* movement in Korea. Through struggle against the feudal social system in Korea and armed with the ideology "humanity is heaven," the oppressed *minjung* began to define themselves as subjects, rather than objects, of history and destiny.

Also during the Yi Dynasty, bands of armed peasants called *Hwalbindang* rose up in every part of the country. The social ideal that they possessed came from a story written by Ho-Kyun about Hong Kil Dong. Ho-Kyun was a *chungin* (member of the social class between the ruling *yang ban* class and the commoners). He wrote this popular story in the *Hangul* so that the *minjung* could read it easily. The story was told and retold and was most popular during the Yi Dynasty, when the ruling powers were making the *minjung* suffer most.[13]

The story of Hong Kil Dong is as follows: An alienated social hero named Hong Kil Dong leaves home and joins a group of bandits because he cannot fulfill his life's ambitions and goals in the existing society. Collecting a gang around him he names it *Hwalbindang* (party to liberate the poor and oppressed). The hero of the story attacks the rich and distributes wealth to the poor *minjung.* This creates great social disturbances. Finally, the hero is persuaded by his father to leave the country, and he goes off to an island called Yuldo, which is his paradise. It is characterized by the absence of social and class divisons.

With its picture of a messianic kingdom, the novel prompted a new social vision among the people. Just like the hero in the story, the *Hwalbindang* in Korea were concerned with national rights and equality of all. Driven by the desire to eliminate the gap between the rich and the poor, they too robbed the rich in order to help the poor.[14]

Meanwhile, after the crushing of the *Tonghak* Rebellion (1895) by the government, the countryside was wide open for missionary penetration. Missionaries went deep into the countyside and made contacts with the *minjung* who were associated with *Tonghak* movement. Christianity was then accepted by the *minjung* as a tool for fighting for justice, equality, and human rights. Christianity became a politically oriented faith and a religion of hope and power for the oppressed and suffering *minjung*.

During this period the major emphasis of Korean Christianity was to achieve equality of human beings and to assure human rights and social justice for the Korean people. The *minjung* became enlightened and inspired, and they were stirred up against the administration and illegal acts of government officials. An important part of the Korean Christian movement was the "common meeting," at which a cross section of the *minjung* voiced their common concerns. [15] The common meetings also engendered a new *minjung* leadership. For instance, after attending the meetings a butcher (whose occupation was classified as *xiang rom*) named Park Song-chun became a Christian and later went on to lead the Butchers' Liberation Movement from 1895 to 1898 and to become one of the founding members of the Seungdong Presbyterian church in Seoul.[16] These common meetings spread throughout the countryside. Since the missionaries had to travel to reach the *minjung*, they had to train more Korean Christian leaders who could go with them. Thus Dr. Samuel A. Moffett founded a theological institutiion (which is now the Presbyterian College and Seminary) in 1901.

The missionaries gradually ceased to be pioneers and to preach directly to the *minjung*. They became organizers or managers, directing and supervising the Korean Christians' evangelical enterprise. They would make occasional trips into the countryside, visiting newly established churches and administering sacraments. The Korean churches used the *Hangul* Bible widely as a very important tool for evangelizing Korea. The Bible became the greatest factor in evangelization.

The Korean churches derived their power, spirituality, great faith in prayer, and liberality from the fact that all the churches were saturated with a knowledge of the Bible. Bible study and training classes constituted the most unique and most important factor in the growth of the Korean churches. [17]

The *minjung* in Korea responded to the Christian message. The motives and reasons for the response, in great measure, were to improve their social and political condition. This was true particularly after 1895. Certainly the Christian message gave some hope to the *minjung,* the outcasts. Political oppression was another cause of the increase in believers. The *minjung* felt that they had reached the summit of misery.

The year 1905 was a fateful year for the Korean people. That year Korea lost its independence and became a protectorate of Japan. The treaty of the protectorship robbed the kingdom of Korea of its diplomatic rights to deal with foreign powers, for the Japanese established the office of governor general under the Korean king to control the Korean government. For the Korean people this meant that their historical situation now provided a new external focus. Independence and the expulsion of Japanese power from Korea became the main concern of the Korean people. [18]

In the political arena, Korean Christians were not exempt from a sense of national crisis and national humiliation, and they harbored an intense anti-Japanese feeling. The missionaries also felt keenly the estrangement between the Koreans and the Japanese which seemed to presage a general uprising. However, they not only understood the hopelessness of fighting against the Japanese imperial army, but also foresaw the danger of making the young Korean churches a political agency. It seems that missionaries were successful in depoliticizing the Korean Christians through mass revival meetings. The main features of the several Protestant revival meetings held in 1907 were the confession of sins after a sermon convincing the people of their sins, loud prayers, and various forms of collective emotional expressions. These revival meetings brought a deep sense of fellowship among Christian communities and a moral transformation of individual lives. However, the Christian message was no longer geared to the social and national crisis of the Korean *minjung,* but was limited to the rigid and narrow definition of salvation of the soul. The Korean Christians' aspiration for national liberation was completely ignored, and the missionaries' tight control of the Korean Christian communities stifled the dynamism of the autonomous communities which could have responded better to the historical predicament.

August 29, 1910, was a day of national humiliation for the Korean people. This was the day that Korea was formally annexed to Japan. The Korean people lost their country and became enslaved *minjung* subjected to the Japanese military rule. The Yi Dynasty formally ended and the right of government was transferred to the Japanese emperor.

The Japanese government strongly infused the policy of Japanese ultranationalism into Korea. According to that policy, all values and institutions came under the imperial authority of the emperor. Hence, the government, the military, business, and all truth, beauty, and morality were linked to the institution of emperor. The infamous Education Rescript was an open declaration of the fact that the Japanese state, being a religious, spiritual, and moral entity, claimed the right to determine all values. This was the spirit of Japanese national policy. It was combined with the doctrine of the divinity of the emperor, a belief championed by the Japanese military, which was the holy army of the emperor and which had launched the mission of bringing the "light of the emperor" to Korea. [19]

For the Korean Christians, political neutrality was not possible whether they were in the churches or outside of them. The oppression, exploitation, and alienation by the Japanese government of the Koreans became extraordinarily cruel. Physical tortures and imprisonments were common practices. Living under the oppressive Japanese rule meant inevitable suffering for powerless Koreans, the *minjung* of the time.

Under the extreme conditions of political oppression, economic exploitation, social alienation by a foreign regime, and internal control by the missionaries, the Korean Christians had no positive outlet to express their feelings and aspirations other than in dreams, but dreams were powerful forces for the people's historical self-understanding. In their dreams, Korean Christians found the God of the Exodus most meaningful for their historical condition. For example, a preface to a Sunday school lesson from this period states:

The Book of Exodus is written about the powerful God, who liberated the people of Israel [which would have been interpreted as meaning the Korean people] from suffering and enslavement and made them the people who enjoyed glorious freedom; God appeared as Yahweh before Israel, and as the whole and just God. God exists by himself and of himself, God has sympathy, and God is the Saviour. Exodus is the book of the miracle of God's liberation of the people of Israel from the power of Pharaoh [the Japanese emperor] with God's power. God has saved Israel first and established it as holy. This book is a foreshadowing of the redemptive love of Jesus in the Gospels and of God's power that cleanses; that is, the miracle of the grace shown forth. [20]

The struggles of the Korean Christians for independence and social justice were persistent despite the regulation concerning meetings (1910) and that concerning guns and explosives (1912). The continuing efforts of the Korean Christians became the spiritual backbone of the March First Independence Movement of 1919. From 1896 to 1898 many intellectuals, merchants, and industrialists had organized the Independence Association. With the help of the *minjung* who participated in the *Tonghak* Rebellion in 1895, the Independence Association formed a society which later provided two main leaders of the March First Independence Movement. These people had the consciousness of the struggle of the *minjung* for liberation. Perhaps this movement was the broadest in scope of the *minjung* liberation movement. Of the people who constituted the movement, 48 percent were peasants, 22 per cent were Christians, and 30 percent were ordinary men and women in their twenties. Christians provided much of the leadership of this movement. Unfortunately, the March First Independence Movement was crushed by the Japanese imperial army.

The missionaries in this period were products of early twentieth-century fundamentalism, and their only concern was the "salvation of souls." Also, in order to do their mission work, they found it necessary to collaborate with the Japanese authorities. However, these relationships changed as World War II approached and began, and toward the end of World War II, the missionaries were expelled from Korea, leaving the Korean churches to carry on their mission by themselves. We may characterize the Korean church between 1920 and

1945 in the following manner: (1) It lacked a historical consciousness. (2) It yielded to the enforcement of worship at the Japanese shrine (Shintoism). (3) It was under the sway of fundamentalistic dogma and imported theology. (4) It became a captive to those who were striving for ecclesiastical authority. This was the period of the "Egyptian Captivity" of the Korean church's history.

The Koreans did not see their liberation until the end of World War II in 1945. It was at this time that they finally were liberated from the rule of the Japanese emperor who, like Pharaoh, had exploited them to the utmost. Thus, the Exodus Model parallels the Korean experience in many ways. The *minjung* of Korea, like the Hebrews, had to assume responsibility and strengthen their awareness of the depths of their bondage in order to rise up against the system in rebellion. In other words, the *minjung* in Korea were actively participating in the process of their own liberation, fully aware that God stood with them and for them.

Furthermore, in the context of the Exodus event, the *minjung* can be clearly understood as a force that stands in opposition to the powerful. The *minjung* are the oppressed who have their rights infringed upon by rulers. They are "uprooted people" who have no national indentity or legal protection and who are considered to be slaves. In Korea, the pattern of slavery, like that experienced by the Hebrews in Egypt, was not questioned and was considered reasonable by those who benefited from the social system. A slave society had long been accepted as the natural and unchangeable order of things. In both Egypt and Korea, while the government leaders regarded the subjected people as a most important element in their economy, they never considered giving them fair compensation for their work. Finally, the Hebrews, being the objects of God's liberation, cried out to God for liberation from the oppressive and unjust Egyptian society. These cries reflected the same aspirations as those of the *han*-ridden *minjung* in Korea.

The Hebrews in
Premonarchical Canaan

As we turn back to the Old Testament once again, we will now explore the experience of the Hebrew people as they arrived in the promised land, Canaan. There are three theoretical models used by scholars to describe this process of settlement, two of which will be explained here in brief, while the other will be used more fully in our discussion.

The Conquest Model is the oldest of the three models and superficially is in line with the traditional claim of the Old Testament as set forth in the Book of Joshua. The Old Testament claims that the twelve tribes of Israel joined in a concerted campaign to conquer and destroy the inhabitants of Canaan. The major biblical narratives that deal with the conquests of Canaanite territories are the capture of Jericho (Josh. 6), the capture of Ai (Josh. 8), the client treaty with Gibeon, Chepherah, Beeroth, and Kiriathjearim subordinated to Israel (Josh. 9), the capture of Makkedah, Linah, Lachish, Eglon, Hebron, and Debir (Josh. 10), and the capture of Hazor (Josh. 11). In this way, Joshua defeated the entire land and all the kings (Josh. 10:40), leaving the Hebrews free from serious opposition.

However, contradictions to this model arise when the whole body of biblical and extrabiblical data is carefully examined. First of all, the Joshua accounts weaken when we look at the archaeological evidence concerning Jericho, Ai, and Gibeon. If Jericho stood at all in the late thirteenth century, it would certainly have been no more than a small walled settlement. Ai (et-Tell) was not occupied at that time and had not been occupied for centuries. Moreover, the biblical Ai has not been located in the area around et-Tell.[1] There have been no Late Bronze remains found at Gibeon except some tomb pottery from the fourteenth and possibly early thirteenth centuries. Furthermore, there is no record of conquest of the following cities: Shiloh (secured at the time of Solomon, 1 Kings 9:16), Jerusalem (secured at the time of David, Judg. 1:21), and other cities built on hills (with the exception of Hazor, which was conquered) (Josh. 11:13). Thus, it is impossible to determine if the Hebrews actually conquered and destroyed all the cities in the land of Canaan in the thirteenth century.[2]

The Migration Model is another model used to describe the settlement of Canaan. It has been widely used by biblical scholars since early in the twentieth century. There are two theories in relation to this model. The first claims that the Hebrews migrated to Canaan in cyclical, seasonal rhythms as seminomads and settled in the empty space between the widely scattered Canaanite city-states. They developed their society there for a period of time without significant contact with the Canaanites. The second theory of the Hebrew migration stresses more contact, the use of treaty relations with the Canaanites, and even some significant mixing of the two peoples. At any rate, according to the Migration Model, the Hebrews peacefully occupied Canaan. If this is true, then it is unlikely that the Hebrews would have destroyed the cities in the late thirteenth and early twelfth centuries.[3]

There are objections to this model as well. First, Judges 1 indicates that there must have been some seizure of land by force. Second, the unity among the Hebrews seems to have been so powerful that any place they moved through would have been completely destroyed. Third, the narrative of the settlement of Canaan does not prove the tradition of the Old Testament—in fact the Old Testament contains a number of contradictions on this subject. This theory thus depends too much on a selective reading of the evidence, causing a lack of agreement even among its proponents.[4]

The third model, the Revolt Model, will be used more thoroughly in our discussion. This model has only recently been advanced and is allied to both preceding models. It is allied to the Conquest Model because the Hebrews are viewed as outsiders who entered into Canaan with a covenantal relation to their liberator God, Yahweh. At the same time, it is allied to the Migration Model because it does not make a sharp distinction between Canaanite and Israelite. However, it appears that the background for the Revolt Model is developed chiefly from the Canaanite city-state, which was mostly a feudal system. This feudal system began in the Hyksos Age (1750-1550 B.C.) and expanded throughout the Egyptian domination of Canaan during the sixteenth and thirteenth centuries.

When the Hebrews entered Canaan, Canaan was politically not a nation-state. Rather, it was a collection of small, walled city-states, each headed by a warlord and each having a population of less than a few thousand people. All were under the domination of the Egyptian emperor who controlled the distribution of all wealth and resources.

The children of warlords were taken to the Egyptian court to be Egyptianized and were held to insure their fathers' good behavior. There was constant petty warfare among these city-states, for with no centralized authority each one existed for itself. At the same time, Egypt claimed all property rights, and taxes were paid to Pharaoh. However, aristocrats were given land which could be inherited by their sons (patrimonial land tenure) in exchange for military service and loyalty. High officials were given land as payment for services (prebendal land tenures). Although officially the land was not to be inherited by their sons, it often became patrimonial nonetheless.

The land itself—the topography, soil, and climate—was suited to a basically agrarian society. Seventy to ninety percent of the people were peasants who were allowed use of land in exchange for 50 percent or more of the produce as taxes. Rulers demanded all surplus crops, leaving the peasants barely enough to stay alive. Merchants benefited from this system as they could accumulate wealth by buying at a low cost from the peasant and then selling to the elite for a large profit. In addition, the Canaanite religion and the priests sanctioned this arrangement in return for economic favors and power in the king's cabinet.

Another important part of the picture of premonarchical Canaan concerned the Canaanites' method of agricultural production. There were two elements: the cereal farmers who tended to work in a centralized system under the control of the warlords, and the herders who, roaming over the rocky hill country with their sheep, worked in a decentralized system. There was an important interdependence between the two groups. In the fall just before rains started, cereal fields were scratch-plowed, and wheat and barley were sown. Then the rains came and, until harvest, there was little need for human labor. These same rains also greened the natural grasses of the steppe region. It was during this period that the flocks of sheep and goats were taken into the hills to graze. This required a large input of human labor. So the labor demand in the herding cycle corresponded to the light demand in the cereal field. In the spring the rains stopped, the weather warmed, and the grass and water supplies in the natural pasture of the hills dried up. The grains had ripened, and the animals were brought back to the ever-flowing springs in the lowlands. Every available person was needed for the cereal harvest. As soon as the fields had been harvested, the animals were turned loose to feed on the stubble—and to spread fertilizer.

Cereal farming and herding were cooperative occupations. The farmer and herder lived side by side—and were often one and the same. They were economically interdependent. This had far-reaching implications on the Hebrew community. One of these was the pressure on the Hebrews to cooperate and join with Canaanite farmers in their fertility celebrations to the gods who gave them rich harvests.

Warlords in Canaan maintained control through their military system. The dominant means of implementing armed force were the chariot and composite bow. The Canaanite chariot was really just a moveable firing platform carrying two men, one of whom would manage the team of horses while the other shot the bow. Obviously, the only persons who could afford to have horses and to hire artisans to build chariots and bows were members of the ruling elite.

Tactically, in the lowlands (where water was ample) were found the walled cities. In the lowlands lived the tiny fraction of the population which had dominant control of the armed forces. But in the uplands, where there were steep valleys and scrub woods, chariots were of little use. In addition, from the standpoint of the ruling elite, there was nothing of use or value in this area to defend.

One thing that helped the peasants in Canaan was the development of a frontier. This gave the peasant family some choice. This sparsely settled raw frontier (primarily the hill country of Canaan) was for those who were considered "outlaws" in the official system.

Among these were social bandits and guerrilla fighters from various marginal sources—all of them were opposed to the monarchy and the elite. They were in the true sense of the word the *habiru* — or *minjung* — in Canaan. In addition, the frontier was exactly where the Hebrews were to be found after the Exodus from Egypt into Canaan. Those who were willing to brave this frontier were those with little to lose, those who had a proclivity for independence and innovation. Having risked their lives, these people of the frontier were not about to hand over their surplus products to anyone.

The *habiru* were the alternative consciousness of Canaan.[5] The Revolt Model puts forth the theory that eventually, unwilling to tolerate continued domination by the ruling class, the *habiru* finally joined in a movement of protest to overthrow the existing system. Whether or not this actually happened is important, for if Canaan was conquered in this way, the *minjung* would have defined themselves as people who take action to determine their own destiny. Refusing to allow themselves to be the objects of oppression, they would have asserted themselves to become *subjects* of history. In order to determine if this was indeed the case, we must first examine the system of government during this time.

The Canaanite city-states were in effect vassals of Egypt. The result of this was a double layer of hierarchical structures, the native rulers subject to the pharaohs and the native populations directly subject to their rulers and indirectly to the Egyptians.

One needs little imagination to understand the powerlessness that a peasant would feel at the very bottom of this hierarchy of domination. The local ruler's power was absolute. The warlord was responsible for both waging war and imposing law. He was the legal power over all the land in the kingdom. Certain loyal subjects received estates in return for service to him. He controlled the transfer of property, settled disputes, and confiscated the property of those who violated his laws. And when the difficulties that Egypt experienced at administering this extended empire resulted in a relaxation of taxation and tribute paid by the local rulers, this respite was not passed on to the lower strata of society. Thus, there seems to be little doubt that conditions for a protest movement existed.

Eventually Egyptian power began to wane, and the declining

strength of the Egyptian dynastic control left a political vacuum in Canaan—a situation that furthered the possibility for revolt. There were cracks and strains in the structure of Canaanite society. The turmoil reached down into the lower levels of society. Rebellious serfs and restive free farmers were also acting the part of *minjung*. In the confused situation created by the diminution of Egyptian control, these lower-class people revolted against those who exploited them.[6] They did this by direct removal of particularly oppressive rulers, by joining forces with another city-state, or by joining a larger movement of revolt—which was precisely the Hebrew people of the Exodus. The stress-torn Canaanite society, in further decline a century after the period described in the Amarna letters, was in need of new leadership:

> The advocates of a revolt model for Israelite origins picture these Israelite tribes as immediate allies of the Canaanite lower classes. Both groups shared a lower-class identity. The former slaves from Egypt, now autonomous, presented an immediate appeal to the restive serfs and the peasants of Canaan.[7]

In addition to their history and experience as liberated slaves, the people of the Exodus had something else to offer. They were united by a theological vision. The theological vision was to have a new social reality under the guidance of the liberator God, Yahweh. This reality included an alternative consciousness which could both criticize the dominant consciousness of the culture and energize the *minjung* with the newness which God had promised. The awareness of the Hebrews that they no longer had to worship the gods of Egypt and could respond to Yahweh free from the political bondage of their situation provided the alternative consciousness and the alternative community witnessed to by Moses. As this consciousness and alternative community emerged, the dominant political power died. The *minjung* were empowered and the powerful oppressors lost their control over the *minjung*. Furthermore, energizing includes the dimension of embracing the darkness and giving witness to a new reality. Considering all these factors, the importance and attraction of Hebrew Yahwism to the oppressed Canaanites can hardly be overestimated. It gave them the final element needed to coalesce the alternative consciousness.[8] Here was a people who had overthrown its oppressors and whose religion celebrated the actuality of deliverance from sociopolitical bondage.

Their strength came from a very specific mandate from their God.

The solidarity of the people of the Exodus was attractive to all Canaanites suffering oppression and subjection to a monopoly of power. In the plains, taxation was heavy — 50 percent or more of produce. As a result of this and other factors, entire clans or tribes joined the newly formed community and identified themselves as Hebrews. This deliverance from bondage was complete when, during the course of time, the small religious community of Israel polarized the existing population throughout the land; some joined, while others fought against them and were defeated.

Thus, the Revolt Model offers a setting which effectively meshes the biblical narratives, the archaeological findings, and the understandings of sociopolitical theory. It offers us a means of understanding the ancient appellation of *habiru* in a way that accounts for its frequent and varied occurrence and its historical identification with the Hebrews. It should be noted that there is by no means universal agreement with either the principle or the details of the Revolt Model. On the contrary, a lively and spirited debate goes on between its adherents and its detractors.

If we accept this model, the parallels with the *minjung* struggle are obvious. When used to look at conflict, the Revolt Model describes the conflict in socioeconomic terms, rather than merely political ones. This perspective is especially pertinent to the Korean situation, for after obtaining liberation from the Japanese in 1945, the Korean *minjung* experienced problems similar to those suffered by the Hebrews after the Exodus.

When the thirty-six years of Japanese rule in Korea ended after World War II, the country was divided — the United States holding the South and the Soviets the North. Prior to 1945, North Korea held the majority of Christians in the undivided country. With the division, however, many of these Christians fled to the South. Of those who remained many suffered persecution. Practically nothing is known of the church or of the activities of Christians in the North today — except in the negative. In other words, what is known is that no church buildings are in use, no public worship is allowed, and no Christian activity is identified. However, unofficial sources indicate that there are gatherings in the homes of Christians, apparently on lines similar to the house-church movement that survived in China through the Cultural Revolution.

As for South Korea, in 1948, with U. S. support, Dr. Syngman Rhee became president of the Republic of Korea. The United States withdrew its military forces from Korea in 1948. Soon afterwards, on June 25, 1950, North Korean forces invaded the Republic of Korea. The Korean War continued until 1953, even though armistice negotiations began in July 1951.

The damage done by the Korean War is inestimable. Casualties were very heavy and much damage was done not only to the country but also to the entire people of Korea. In the South alone, "150,000 people were killed, 250,000 wounded, 100,000 kidnapped to the north, 200,000 missing and several million homeless."[9] The people of Korea suffered tremendously.

Soon after the war, Rhee's regime, with the help of the United States, began to "rebuild" the country. Business investments from the United States poured in, as well as goods and amounts of the money the likes of which many Koreans had never seen. Consequently, members of the ruling elite realized that they could take advantage of this situation, clinging to their power in order to grab some of those fortunes.

In order for us to understand the situation of post-war Korea, it is also necessary for us to point out that although Korea was called a democratic country, the social system was that of a strict bureaucracy. There were, of course, democratic influences that had managed to emerge through the government's efforts, but they did not bring the country close to democracy in its truest sense. The government was actually a restructuring of the rigid Japanese colonialist system into a somewhat more flexible bureaucracy. The new regime of Syngman Rhee chiefly focused on the president, his associates, civil servants, and the army. These were the dominating groups that exerted their power over everyone else.

U.S. aid and business investments were also monopolized by the ruling elite. With this aid the government was supposed to rebuild the country, but instead it was

interested only in increasing and retainiing its wealth, not in in-
vesting in the country's industrial development. As a result, the
growth of small and medium industries was checked and heavy
industry stagnated. Low productions meant shortages, which in
turn meant inflation. Prices rose, but wages and salaries did not
keep pace, while the fall in the real price of rice threatened farmers'
livelihoods. A small rise in the price of rice meant little, for example, when the price of fertilizer rose by 500 percent between 1953 –
1959.[10]

The result was a double layer of hierarchical structures in the economic
system – the Korean ruling powers subject to the almighty U.S. government and business people and the common people directly subject
to the power groups.

Needless to say, apart from the individuals who were closely
connected with the power groups there were, at this time, free citizens
and many thousands of widows, more than one hundred thousand
orphans, and thousands of unemployed urban laborers (along with the
low paid laborers), farmers, and refugees from the North. These people
were *minjung* who often lived on a near starvation level. Their houses
had been destroyed by the war; upon the debris they built small shacks
to live in. Many refugees lived in refugee camps and school buildings. In
the urban areas, especially among the unemployed, meagre amounts of
food were handed out. Meanwhile, many young widows and girls
became prostitutes for the American soldiers; many orphans with
mixed blood were born because of this, which only added to the
existing orphan problems. Young boys had to become shoeshine boys
and houseboys for the U.S. soldiers. Farmers also had a difficult time
because as they harvested, their crops were taken away by the Korean
soldiers who were stationed in the area. These soldiers, too, had a very
difficult time. Their officers robbed them of their rations, which the
officers then sold in order to further accumulate wealth.

Thus, the entire society was being propelled toward a breaking
point. The power holders were becoming richer and the *minjung*
were becoming poorer. The corruption and injustice practiced against
the *minjung* were unbearable. Soon, their accumulated *han* began to
surface and they began to take revenge against the government of Rhee.

In the meantime, many Christians from the North exercised their
faith. They firmly believed that the God who brought them liberation

from the oppression of the Japanese colonialists and the communist dictators would liberate them from the injustices and corruption of Rhee's regime. They began to establish new churches where they gathered to talk about their family situations and expressed their hope of liberation. They also began talking about prophetic messages against social disorder and corruption in society.

Inspired by these Christians, many university students, discharged soldiers, and other *minjung* joined forces to show their anger and resentment in street demonstrations against the government. These demonstrations culminated on April 19, 1960, when students and many other *minjung* marched in the streets of Seoul to show their dissatisfaction with the handling of the government. Rhee's riot police were ordered to shoot the demonstators on sight, and so they fired on the students as they were reaching the capitol building. There was much bloodshed, which eventually led to the fall of Rhee's regime. Obviously, this student revolt was an example of the *minjung* movement, and it was inspired by the ideals of equality, justice, liberty, and democracy that were taught by Korean Christians.

Thus, it seems that in both the Old Testament and in Korea events occurred as outlined in the Revolt Model. As we proceed through the Old Testament and Korean history simultaneously, the identification of the *minjung* as *actors* becomes increasingly clear. The *minjung* are awakening to the fact that they have the collective power to control their own destiny. They have become more conscientized, more aware of their rightful place in society, and are able to act with the organization and confidence needed to achieve the justice they seek. Indeed, more and more, they are becoming subjects of history.

4.

Solomon, the Creator of
the Victims of Social Injustices

An important lesson emerged out of the triumphs experienced by the *minjung* in Canaan. This lesson was reflected in the Korean experience; that is, although liberation from an oppressive system may be obtainable, building a just and equal society to replace it is not so easily achieved. Indeed, both the Hebrews and the Koreans found out that even after liberation there will always be those who, overcome by greediness, wish to take advantage of the rebuilding process to establish themselves as rulers. These people will force their way to the top of the system, once again subjugating their brothers and sisters in the process. Soon the newly achieved equality is eroded; unjust social structures are introduced; these structures become increasingly hardened, bureaucratic, and dehumanizing; and the *minjung* find themselves back at the bottom. In other words, the greediness of humans is an important aspect in considering the process of liberation, for it was, in fact, what prevented the formation of a just and equal society in Israel after the Exodus as well as in Korea in 1961.

Soon after the Exodus and settlement of the Hebrews in Canaan, David became the leader of the nation of Israel. In this period a new theological rendering of history was effected, its emphasis not on freedom and justice, but on order, stability, and continuity. The alternative consciousness embodied in the Mosaic covenant, once so central to the history of Israel, was replaced by a royal consciousness. This monarchical consciousness, which can be identified in the Davidic covenant, gave credibility to the royal lineage of David. David's line became traceable in two ways—into the past as well as into the future.

Placing him in the lineage of Abraham and Noah legitimated his king-ship, while Yahweh's covenant with the people, God's promises of blessing and prosperity to Israel, now appeared to be channeled through David and his house. And the royal line extended into the future as the Messiah was projected to be a descendant of David.

All of these tendencies heightened under the rule of Solomon, a reign characterized by increased bureaucracy and oppression and perhaps best symbolized by the Temple. His reign clearly exemplified the corruption of leaders by greed and self-interest. Solomon played a significant role in the movement away from the kingdom of equality and toward a kingdom of rulers. He was an oppressive ruler whose political policies resulted in oppression and poverty for most of the Israelites.

At the same time, Solomon's reign made several gains. The living standard in Israel rose. The government employed thousands of people and stimulated private enterprise, thus raising the purchasing power of the entire nation and inducing a general prosperity. Cities grew and new ones were built.[1] Israel enjoyed unexampled prosperity. The nation was militarily secure and there was a material abundance such as Israel had never dreamed of before and never knew existed. As a result, the arts flourished. Literature, psalmody, and music achieved new levels of excellence during the reign of Solomon.

Red Sea trade brought to Israel exotic products: gold, silver, rare woods, jewels, and ivory. Caravan trade with Arabia brought added income. Copper mines produced an ample supply which could be exported in exchange for foreign products. Solomon also acted as the middleman between trade for Cilician horses and chariots from Egypt. Because horses and chariots were the strongest military wea-pons of the eighth century B.C., this important trade was extremely profitable.[2]

At this point, the glory of Solomon ends. From the perspective of *minjung* theology, the advancements that were made in his reign were achieved at considerable cost to Israel. Solomon violated Hebrew tradition in several ways.

The first of these violations was the manner in which Solomon assumed the kingship. Hebraic leadership had always been based on charisma. Tradition legitimated a new king by means of a prophetic oracle. However, this was not so with Solomon. Birth and political influence made him king.[3] His oppressive political policy resulted in the execution of Adonijah, the exile of Abiathar to Anthoth, and the murder of Joab at the altar. Thus it was that the kingdom was established at the hand of Solomon.

Furthermore, Solomon conducted a seven-year program for building the Temple. The Temple was built by Phoenician architects and consequently represented an invasion of Canaanite culture into the center of Israel's life and worship. For example, a number of Canaanite symbols were employed: the bronze sea symbolized the underground freshwater ocean, the source of life and fertility; the altar of burnt offerings suggested the mountain of the gods. The Temple was also politicized when it became the royal chapel, with the chief priest being a royal appointee and a member of Solomon's cabinet.

God now became entrapped, entombed by the temple priests and regulations, no longer free to move with God's people wherever they went. Moreover, God could now be encountered only indirectly and through various mediators. The direct experience of a dynamic God acting in history was lost. God became quarantined in the temple precincts, a "temple God" walled up in the designated place of worship and in a myriad of rules and regulations, all carefully attended to and interpreted by the royal priests. In other words, over the centuries Israel's liberator became domesticated.[4] And as God became entrapped, likewise God's people became entrapped; the interrelationship between theology and social patterns continued to hold. Solomon's reality was characterized by affluence for the few and poverty for the many. The Temple was constructed on the backs of slave laborers and the taxes drawn from the peasants. Consumption replaced covenant as Yahweh and justice took a back seat to pleasures and luxuries, again enjoyed by only a few. Forced labor and oppression reigned, and the people were victimized by injustice and social structures that preyed on the powerless. The irony of all this, once again, was that this was the very thing that the *habiru* had revolted against and escaped from some three centuries before. Only this time it was not Egypt and foreign pharaohs but Israel and its own rulers who were the oppressors.

Solomon also supervised extensive building in Jerusalem as he developed a palace complex which took thirteen years to complete.

Government buildings, the king's house, and the house for his Egyptian queen were part of the huge complex. Outside Jerusalem, Solomon built cities that were garrisons for chariots and other fortifications at Gezer, Megiddo, Hazor, and elsewhere.[5]

As king, Solomon also changed the military structure of Israel. David had maintained two armies: a people's militia and the political army. Solomon did away with the militia and strengthened the professional army. He developed a chariot army whose major responsibility was to protect the land and control the trade routes among Phoenicia, Egypt, Arabia, and elsewhere. John Bright estimates Solomon had 4000 stalls for horses, 1400 chariots, and 12,000 men to operate them. Solomon also maintained a standing army. To operate such a military program, a military aristocracy developed for the first time in Israel's history.[6]

As a result of these projects, the state faced a dilemma. In addition to the building projects and the military, administration of the state required a large bureaucracy. Three thousand and three hundred people were needed just to supervise work programs. To finance the state, Solomon established twelve administrative districts. Each was responsible for supporting the court for one month of the year. This was an enormous strain on districts, for each one averaged scarcely one hundred thousand people. And the real injustice of the administrative districts was that they centralized power by replacing the old tribal system with districts under the supervision of royal appointees instead of tribal elders.

Even this plan was insufficient to bring in the needed government finances, and, consequently, further exploitation was enacted. An example of this was the institution of the hated *corvee*. Although Israel had used foreigners and war captives as slaves, it had never mistreated them, nor had Israel ever used Hebrews as slaves. The *corvee* changed this. Slave labor was used in mining and smelting operations in the Arabah. Because the mortality rate of the slaves was so high, Solomon dared not use Israelites there. Instead, Israelites were used in the logging operations in Lebanon. Over 30,000 were conscripted and worked one month out of every three. Another 80,000 were put to work in stone quarries, while 70,000 more toiled as bearers of various materials.[7]

Solomon used another method to finance his government. Certain towns near the Bay of Acre were given to Hiram I of Tyre, either sold outright or used as collateral against a cash loan that was never redeemed.

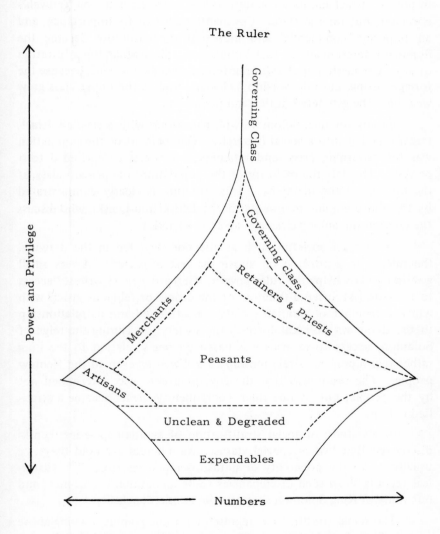

Graphic representation of the relationship among classes in agrarian societies.[8]

It was in these ways that the administration of King Solomon transformed Israel. The tribal confederacy, with its sacred institutions and charismatic leadership, was broken. In its place, a family monarchy, under which all phases of national life were organized, was in power. Israel and its social duties were no longer based on Yahweh's covenant, but on the state. Covenantal law lost its importance, and an imposing commercial and industrial superstructure became the dominant determinant of social obligation. Meanwhile, the infiltration of large Canaanite populations reinforced class distinctions, because the foreign people did not worship Yahweh. And as the upper class grew wealthier, the gap between rich and poor grew.

Because of this, Solomon, who had begun with a classless Israel, transformed it into a social hierarchy. One percent of the population was the governing class, and retainers and priests comprised 3 to 5 percent. This left the majority of the population, the peasant class, at the bottom of the hierarchy. This structure is clearly demonstrated by the above graphic representation by Lenski and Lenski, who discuss the relationship among classes in agrarian societies.

In agrarian societies such as the one depicted in the drawing, the ruler is in a position far above the rest of society. A very small governing class helps the ruler govern. Gerhard Lenski writes, "access to rewards [is] often a function of the ethnic or religious group with which a member of agrarian society was affiliated and its relationship to the dominant political force in the society."[9] During the reign of Solomon, access to rewards was based on one's relation to the king rather than upon one's relationship to Yahweh or even to the Hebrew people. The result was that the governing elite was determined not by the people, but by one ruler; consequently, Israel became a stratified nation.

In his study of social stratification of agrarian societies, Lenski discovered that "when special statuses were hereditary (and they . . . usually were) the possibility of status discrepancies arose."[10] Historical records show such discrepancies to be a common occurrence, and our study of King Solomon supports the Lenski conclusion.

The social stratification represented in the graphic drawing above is not absolute. Mobility between classes in an agrarian culture is possible. Gerhard Lenski presents three factors which can determine vertical mobility in society.[11] First, dominance of a single ruler over the governing class increases the rate of movement into and out of the governing class, whereas oligarchy probably would increase the rate of mobility into and out of the ruler's office. In other words, royal power tends to increase with tenure, and a king—with no checks or balances on his power—can move people up and down the social ladder at whim. Indeed, this is what happened during the rule of Solomon. He was the only ruler; he had a long, secure tenure in office; and he determined who entered the governing class.

Second, wars, famines, and other disasters tend to increase the rate of upward mobility. These same factors reduce downward mobility. As we have seen, such disasters did not occur in Solomon's time. Consequently, one source of social mobility was removed.

Third, the opening of new economic opportunities, especially in the area of trade and commerce, increases the rate of upward movement into the merchant class in the short run, and into the governing class in the long run. Conquest of new territories opens new political opportunities which, in turn, increase the rate of movement into the governing and retainer classes. It was this lack of territorial conquest that closed off another source of upward social mobility during Solomon's time. There were new economic opportunities and, in the short run, they allowed formation of a merchant class in Israel. However, the huge building programs, the governmental administrative costs, and military expenses simply consumed the profit from commercial enterprises during Solomon's term in office. Thus, a third source of social mobility was eliminated.

The conclusion was inevitable. The political, economic, and religious decisions made by Solomon increased the social stratification in Israel. Truly it was a situation in which the gap between the rich and the poor was widened. As a result, Solomon as a king was totally secure in the land which he had obtained for himself, totally committed to keeping his land on his own terms, and insensitive to the cry of the *han*-ridden people of Israel. He was no better than the Pharaoh of the Exodus narrative.

Needless to say, during his reign Solomon did much to increase the exploitation of the group which the prophet Micah later called "my people": the *minjung,* the victims of social injustice. Certainly, the *corvee* workers, foreigners, enslaved prisoners of war, laborers working in the logging operations and stone quarries, and people in the lower social stratum — such as the unclean, degraded, and expendables — became the *minjung* of Israel. These *minjung* were politically, economically, socially, and culturally oppressed. Alienated by the existing social system, they were reduced to objects of those who held power, becoming mere tools for them. Whatever contribution they made to society gave credit only to Solomon. The *minjung* themselves remained nameless.

All of this came about because of the greed of Solomon. And as a result, the vision of an equal and just society was not realized in Israel. Instead, the new leaders proved to be just as oppressive as the old ones, and the *minjung* found themselves suffering once more. Here, once again, the situation mirrors that of the Korean experience after the ousting of Syngman Rhee. As we shall now see, greed again played an important role in spoiling the *minjung's* chance for equality.

After Syngman Rhee was forced to resign in 1960, the new national assembly named Dr. Chang Myon prime minister. His government was ousted in a military coup in May 1961. Then the political atmosphere drastically changed. After two years of military government under General Park Chung Hee, civilian rule was restored with the advent of the Third Republic in 1963. Of course, Park was elected president.

In October 1972, one year after he was re-elected for the third time, Park proclaimed a national emergency. He initiated a series of reforms to cope with the domestic and international situation, including an amendment to the constitution enabling him to run the country for another six years.

On October 26, 1979, Park was assassinated and Choi Kyu Hah became president. Although the true power was held by General Chun Doo Hwan, Choi released political detainees and promised a series of political reforms. Student demonstrations turned to violence and there was a major insurrection in Kwangju, where unofficial reports indicated that more than twelve hundred innocent civilians and students were murdered by government soldiers. Choi resigned on August 15, 1980, clearing the way to power for General Chun Doo Hwan, who was elected president on August 27, 1980.

Both of these presidents, Park and Chun, are modern-day equivalents of the Old Testament's Solomon. Their greed and desire to maintain their own personal power at any cost remind us of the problems of Solomon's reign. This similarity is even more evident when we look at the social and economic situation under the Park and Chun regimes.

During these two regimes, there was very rapid economic growth in Korea. The basis of this high growth was a heavy dependence upon foreign capital and technology. The main axes of the growth were in labor-intensive, export-oriented industries. The factories in Korea have been aimed at efficient production of commodities so as to make export profits for national as well as multinational companies. Because of the specialization of jobs and of other demands of mass production, technical growth has occurred in Korea to the point where most men and women in factories are virtually bound to the machines or conveyors they operate. They find little or no creative activity in their labor. Since the workers perform a limited number of strength-consuming operations during their work day, with little change in pace or performance, they suffer from, among other things, severe fatigue. As we all know, one consequence of this fatigue is industrial accidents. And in many cases, there is no type of compensation for these accidents and no implementation of labour laws.

As stated above, many of these factory workers are women, especially young women between fifteen and twenty-one years of age. Low wages for these women have been justified by employers on the grounds that the work they do is temporary, held only until marriage. In reality, however, they have been the objects of much discrimination in a society that is filled with the Confucianist influence. Most of these women have migrated to the urban areas from rural farming areas because they have thought that opportunity and economic gains in the urban areas would bring them new prosperity. But the fact is that they find many problems instead, not only in terms of low wages but also in the areas of housing and vocational skills. Their housing is substandard and their living conditions indicate that they have been exploited and utilized as machines. All of this has brought about their dehumanization. Such an emphasis on industrialization—at the expense of humanization—in economic strategy has brought about imbalance, dependence, and many other serious problems. And as for the *minjung,* this has meant increasingly oppressive economic policies.

For the sake of progress, the government has destroyed most of the ancient houses and has replaced them by ugly cement high-rise buildings. All of the villages, under the New Village Movement, were organized in such a way that the main political party could maneuver the people for the benefit of its political power. And for publicity's sake, the government offers some help to rebuild bridges and dams for irrigation. The fact that many rural people have to migrate to the urban areas to find industrial jobs indicates that these projects have not been sufficient to improve rural life.

Furthermore, because the development process has been dominated by the government, the centralization of power has increased. The consequent low-wage policy for laborers and low-price policy for agricultural products has brought about a strong discontent among the *minjung,* which in turn has brought about political repression instead of democratic political development for Korea. Serious social problems have also arisen, such as a widening gap between the rich and the poor, a deepening of the socioeconomic gap between the rural and the urban areas, rapid urbanization, massive migration of the rural population into urban centers, especially Seoul, sacrifice of the rights and welfare of workers, and ecological disruption. Cultural values have been restricted by a loss of the freedom of speech and publication, which has been caused by the concentration of power in the hands of a few. The final result of all of this has been the wide-scale suppression of intellectual freedom.

Corrupt politics in itself has long been regarded as a pressing social problem in Korea. The political parties, with their bosses, graft, and business-political and criminal-political interrelationships have received the *minjung's* moral condemnation. Furthermore, since the government has complete control over the media, it is able to brainwash the ordinary Korean people into accepting and praising the present economic and political policy of the country. Thus, the *minjung* no longer understand what is going on in the country. The news that one hears from the government and the rumors that one hears from reliable sources tell different stories. And it would not be incorrect to say that about 80 percent of the rumors are more accurate than the news itself.

In order to further publicize that the nation is in good shape, the government has built many high-rise buildings in the Seoul area. The government has brought many international meetings to Korea. Its most highly acclaimed accomplishment was obtaining the privilege of hosting the 1986 Asian Games and the 1988 Summer Olympiad. But the question is: At whose expense are all these beautiful buildings being erected? The answer, of course, is the *minjung.*

The government is also hosting presidential prayer breakfasts and is granting many favors to religious leaders, especially the fundamentalist church leaders. This has given many priests and pastors the opportunity to secure tax-free property and enjoy a standard of living equal to or exceeding that of the upper class. They have built large religious buildings and magnificent church facilities which are beautifully decorated with flowers and other ornaments that praise the "holy, holy . . . God" who is supposedly present in these holy places which humans have constructed. Many pastors.are saying, "Come to *our* church, which is the only true 'conservative' church and meet your God who is present only in this church, because we believe nothing but the Bible." Theologically, this means that God has become a prisoner in that particular church. The idea of an omnipresent and free God has been taken away. Furthermore, during this time, the leaders of the Korean Protestant churches have been overwhelmingly fundamentalistic, sectarian, ritualistic, and formalistic. Most Protestant churches have not changed their beliefs, attitudes, and theologies for sixty years (1920-1980). In spite of significant contributions toward self-awareness and nationhood by the churches, the majority of the leaders have not been influenced by the contemporary trends of the world church. Furthermore, the feeling of repression which had occurred during the Japanese occupation has continued to dominate the mood of the church even after the liberation of the nation. The church has lacked a guiding concept in a changing world, due to the fact that strong foreign influences have been present. As a result, an indigenous theology has been developed.

Meanwhile, the fact that fundamentalism is primarily oriented toward "the other world" and "salvation of souls" has discouraged any meaningful social involvement of the churches. Because of this, the Korean churches have been alienated from society, and have contributed very little or nothing at all toward the furthering of social justice. Nevertheless, the Christian community has grown, and the estimated total church membership has reached eight million, many of whom are refugees from North Korea.

In order to justify the unjust system in Korea, the government protects and rationalizes the ruling political party, multinational as well as national corporations, and large churches. In order to justify these institutions as having been approved by God, government and church officials are fond of quoting Romans 13:1-7, which states that "every person [should] be subject to the governing authorities." *Minjung* theologians, on the other hand, maintain that the essential teaching of the Bible is the ceaseless protest against tyrannical governments. They turn for support to Ephesians 6:11-12, which calls on us to "Put on the whole armor of God, that [we] may be able to stand against the wiles of the devil. For we are not contending against flesh and blood, but against the principalities, against the powers, against the world rulers of this present darkness, against the spiritual hosts of wickedness in the heavenly places." This polarizing created by conflicting ways of interpreting the Bible creates tense situations which do not allow for an interchange of ideas.

It is now clear then that, here again, there are parallels between the Koreans under Park and Chun and the Israelites under Solomon's reign. Like the entrapment of God in Solomon's Temple, the entrapment of God in the fundamentalist teachings of the Korean Protestant churches has caused stagnation in the churches' contribution to social justice. Furthermore, like Solomon, Park and Chun both quickly seized power and immediately started a rebuilding process aimed at pushing the nation forward militarily, economically, and culturally. This, however, has come at the cost of the Korean *minjung,* who have become the tools of those in power. And, finally, the same greed and hunger to stay in power that drove Solomon to disregard the rights of the Hebrew people has caused the suppression of human rights in Korea that continues today.

5.

Prophets
and the Helpless,
Poor, and Oppressed

Out of the oppression that occurred during and after Solomon's reign, a new figure arose to challenge the existing order. The *han*-ridden cries of the *minjung* found their voice in these spokespersons. The voice was that of the prophets. In a masterful way these figures became the conscientizers of the people. In other words, they unmasked that which was false among the royal families and appealed to the royal consciousness while being situated in the reality of the *minjung*. They did not speak of the distance of a remote future, but they spoke of the socio-economic and political situation of the time. If we are to understand the nature of prophecy, we must also understand the feelings of the prophets and their connection with the people.

Amos was the first prophet to rise to prominence at that time. Over the years there has been controversy over the economic status of Amos. Although the traditional view has been that Amos was a poor shepherd, this is probably not true. In fact, one scholar has stated that "Amos was no doubt among the prominent men of the place."[1] At any rate, Amos was neither a professional prophet nor a cult functionary. He received his education from his travels and through association with Edomites and other tribes from the east whose wisdom and knowledge he learned and shared. Amos also acquired instruction in the form of clan wisdom from the elders in the gate at Tekoa.[2]

The Book of Amos states that the prophet was a herdsman and dresser of sycamore trees (7:14) who was called by Yahweh out of the southern kingdom, from Tekoa. Yahweh took him away from tending his flock, ordering him to "Go, prophesy to my people Israel" (7:15).

Thus, around 750 B.C., Amos traveled to Israel. He went to proclaim God's message of judgment and the imminent end of Israel.

To whom does Amos direct his message? Obviously, he addressed his message to the people of Israel. In studying the Book of Amos, we discover that he employs the special term "my people Israel," a phrase he uses three times in the book. By looking at Amos's use of the phrase "my people Israel" we can draw three conclusions. First, he is refer- ring only to the northern kingdom of Israel. Second, by this term he designates a particular group or class within northern Israel, and he indicates that God's judgement will fall upon the religious elite, the rulers, and the upper class of Israel. Third, this term includes the oppressed and needy of northern Israel, but it excludes them from God's judgment and punishment. God's judgment is not all-inclusive but discriminating. There is a distinction between those who will be judged and those who will be spared divine punishment.

The rulers, upper class, and religious elite are the ones who will be judged by God. In today's language, they are the strong, the well-to-do, the well-housed, the well-fed, the authorities, and the holders of power and privilege. They are the oppressors and the ex- ploiters of the *minjung*. Like Solomon, they are the creators of social injustices.

Amos's denouncement of the ruling elite points to one basic injustice, namely oppression. This includes the selling of slaves, plun- der, excessive taxation and rent rates, and demands for payment to the last grain of wheat. In addition, the prophet's denouncement includes those of the ruling class who conspire to ignore or silence the pleas of the *minjung*, often taking bribes; who promote a corrupt marketing system, always to the peasants' disadvantage; and who have turned over the already scarce land to the cultivation of luxury crops such as olives and grapes.

As for the marginal and oppressed people of northern Israel, Amos uses three key Hebrew words to identify them. He refers to them as the "helpless" in 2:7, 4:1, 5:11 and 8:6; the "poor" in 2:6, 4:1, 5:12, and 6:46; and the "oppressed or afflicted" in 2:7 and 8:14. These are the people for whom Amos has overwhelming compassion and concern.

One of Amos's targets is Samaria, where the majority of the

ruling elite live. The Samarians do not know to do what is right; they store up violence and destruction in their strongholds (3:10). The rich and powerful store up treasures and profits taken from the poor by violence and exploitation. The wealthy continually violate the moral and legal laws of the Mosaic covenantal tradition. Amos cries out, "Hear this word, you Bashan cows on mount Samaria, who oppress the needy, crush the poor, saying to their lords, 'Bring that we may drink' " (4:1).

At this point, we can point out a clear mark of the monarchy condemned by Amos: the economics of affluence.[3] The economics of affluence is made possible by the oppressive social policy. Amos is offended by the affluence and opulence of Israel, because they are achieved at the expense of the poor and needy. The "cows of Bashan on Mount Samaria" refer to members of the elite social class of the capital of northern Israel: the wives of the court officials, of the wealthy proprietors of large estates (5:11-12), and of the merchants (8:4-6).[4] They are the indolent, self-indulgent, and greedy upper-class women who make demands on their husbands to engage in corrupt business practices.

In Amos 5:10-12, the prophet protests the corruption of the legal system. The gate he refers to is a fortified building which was set in the walls of the city and which housed the local courts. The demoralized court system had lost much of its integrity. The circle of witnesses, possibly partly composed of royal administrators and elders, detested the "one who [testified] fully." They abhorred the truth when confronted with it. Judgments and decisions were arrived at through bribes, illegal maneuvering, and assorted dissolute practices. The innocent were found guilty, and the needy were precluded from the legal system.

In Amos 10:11, the prophet declares, "Because you extort rent from the poor and take grain-tax from him, you have built houses of hewn stone, but you shall not dwell in them." Here, Amos refers to the excessive rent-gouging occurring in Samaria. From the time of Solomon, there had been a shift in the socioeconomic system in Israel which gradually pushed peasants off their lands. Peasants were forced to head toward the cities. Those who once owned and worked their own lands were forced into serfdom. The small farmers no longer owned their property; they had to rent almost everything from landlords. The elite landlords often owned not only the land, but the peasants too. When the peasants needed to borrow money, they had to do so at exorbitant rates of interest.

This socioeconomic system, which had become corrupt, was supposed to be monitored at the gate—the seat of the legal system. Rather than fulfilling this function, however, the corrupt courts conspired with the system to perpetuate a socioeconomic system in which the wealthy elite dominated and exploited the lower classes.

Amos does not attack only this corrupt court system; he also attacks Israel's commerce. The poor were being victimized by profiteering and impure business practices. Merchants and proprietors were exploiting the poor in the local marketplace. As James Mays has written of this situation: "In selling grain to the poor these cunning merchants used a small 'peck' to measure what they gave, and a heavy weight to determine what they got."[5]

The above are examples of the oppressive social and economic policies at work in northern Israel. The prophet was outraged by the oppressive and exploitative practices which he saw in the nation's courts, in the lifestyle of the nation's rulers, in commerce, in the debt-slavery institution, and in the political and economic system.

Amos also illustrates how the religious system was corrupted in northern Israel. We have already seen how Yahweh condemned the religion and government of northern Israel. In 7:10-17 we have the historical recollection of a confrontation between Amaziah, the priest of Bethel, and Amos. Amaziah has sent a report to King Jeroboam about the prophesying of Amos. Subsequently, Amaziah orders Amos to return to Judah to do his preaching. The priest tells Amos that the Bethel temple is the king's place of worship; it is a national temple (7:13).

Amos's response to Amaziah demonstrates Amos's courage and unswerving dedication to Yahweh. "Amos speaks out against those who violate the torah—who try to stop the word of God, even if it touches the king."[6] Amaziah, however, believes the monarchy has special religious privileges: "Amaziah does not doubt the authority of the torah but believes the royal reality has immunity."[7] The uncompromising message of Amos is that nobody, including the religious elite, is immune from God's law. Amos declares that the religion of northern Israel is, as are all persons and institutions, accountable solely to the judgment of Yahweh.

Another prophet to rise up at this time out of the social situation in Judah was Micah. Micah made his prophecies in the eighth century B.C., during the time of Amos's upbringing. Moreover, the socio-political situation that Micah addressed was much the same that Amos attacked — the human situation of broken relationships and the systematic dehumanization of the majority by a privileged self-seeking minority through a sophisticated and inescapable economic exploitation was common in Palestine in the days of both prophets. Micah, like Amos, directed his words to the subtle and greedy oppressor and the extravagant reveler. His oracle sounded like thunder. It was short, direct, loud, and clear. It was not a warning; it was a sentence, pronouncing a clear and irreversible execution. His oracle was on behalf of "my people."

One example of this appears in Micah 2:7b-9. Some of the sins of the oppressors which Micah criticized are set forth in these verses:

> But you! Against my people you arise as enemy. From the peaceful their cloak you strip, taking away security, plotting war. You drive the women of my people from their comfortable house. From their children you take their dignity forever.

Here, Micah has singled out two terms in particular: "my people" and "enemy." These terms are to be understood differently from their usual meanings. The concept of "my people," as used by Micah, is in accord with the concept of *minjung,* because it is meant to indicate that the oppressors and the oppressed are members of the same nation. Micah makes a distinction between "my people" and "enemy," though both are from the people of the same nation. Whereas "my people" are always on the side of the prophet, the "enemy" is always on the opposite side. In fact, probably the most outstanding Old Testament example of a conflict between suffering people and the ruling class is found in Micah 2:8.

And who, exactly, does Micah mean when he says "my people"? These people should be understood as the country people who lived in the vicinity of Moresheth, the powerless widows who had lost all their property to the ruling class, and the poor who had been exploited both physically and economically. In a word, "my people" for Micah were the have-nots.

Those who lived in the time of Micah had more freedom in terms of the social structure than those who lived in Amos's time. However, they were also robbed of their houses, land, and labor, not at the hands of another nation as the Hebrews had experienced in Egypt, but rather by their own people, by those who shared a common heritage. In other words, the condition of the people in Micah's time was basically the result of unjust power structures. But Micah does make distinctions among types of exploitation. In Micah 2:2,9 most of the the women and children who were robbed of their houses and land are distinguished from those who were exploited for their labor. We can see that these old widows, the sick, children, and other powerless people roamed like a nomadic people. They could not fend for themselves and were a constant burden to society. Yet all of these were Micah's people.

Let us consider the legal status of Micah's "my people." It is known that, in Micah's time, social law was deeply related to personal avarice. In 3:8, Micah says, "But I! I am filled with power, with Yahweh's spirit, and justice and might." In this passage, judgment as the arm of justice is emphasized. Justice for Micah was a social law which should be observed not only by the high officials in Jerusalem, but also by the judges. In 3:1 Micah insists that justice and righteousness should be observed as law by everyone: "Hear, you heads of Jacob and leaders of the house of Israel! Isn't it your part to know justice?" Micah points out that the ruling class should be the best equipped to know the law, but because they were "haters of good and lovers of evil" (3:2), they do not put justice and righteousness into practice. In 3:9 he says that they "detest justice and pervert the right [way]." The role of the law for Micah is not to promote national development or social order, but to insure freedom from oppression and extortion. He also points out that minority groups should not be ignored because of the prosperity and happiness of the majority.

Thus, "my people" for Micah were those who did not speak of their agony—the *han*-ridden *minjung*—although they had had their property, as well as their freedom, taken from them, We see in 3:3-4 that, in spite of being beaten and brutalized, they remained in silence and did not even appeal to God; rather, it was the thieves who appealed to God.

In 2:6-11 Micah attacks the ruling class and the false prophets.

He says the members of the ruling class devise a false faith and theology to justify their prosperity, security, and happiness — and thus reject the word of God. Their minds are closed not only to God, but also to the true prophet, and they are always thinking of ways to maintain and increase their wealth. We can see this further in 3:5-6:

> This is what Yahweh has said against the prophets who mislead my people, when they have something to chew on, they proclaim "Peace." Let a man fail to put something in their mouth and they sanctify war against him. Therefore, it will be night for you without vision, darkness for you without divination. The sun shall set for the prophets, the day go dark for them.

The false prophets' oracles and the ruling class's false faith are derived from their selfish desire to maintain their property and happiness.

In Micah's time, the false prophets supported the actions of the ruling class without criticism and proclaimed peace to those who gave them a donation or gift. Judgment and war were proclaimed against those who did not give them a bribe. These false prophets lived in Jerusalem, where most of the rich, with their large house and lavish lifestyles, lived.

The prophet Micah, however, was different. He did not stand on the side of the rich but sought out those who sweated and bled in Jerusalem and, in hopes of solving their problems, he went to the public offices in Jerusalem, not in order to live with wealth and power, but to participate in the suffering of the people with whom he lived. He went to find the lost sheep like the good shepherd of the New Testament (John 10:11f.). He did not flee from the sufferings of his people but was drawn to them.

What concrete actions did Micah take on behalf of his nation? In Micah 1:6 and 3:12, we see that he proclaimed judgment on Samaria. Micah foresaw the defeat of the northern kingdom and the fall of Samaria to Assyria. He prophesies the following against Samaria: "I will make Samaria into a ruin in the field, a place to plant vineyards. I will pour her stones into the valley and uncover her foundations."

After the fall of Samaria is proclaimed, Micah begins to mourn. In 1:8f. he proclaims: "Over this I will mourn and wail; I will go stripped and naked. I will raise a mourning like jackals, a grieving like the ostrich, that the wound of God is incurable, that it has come to

Judah. God has reached to the gate of my people, to Jerusalem." It was very important to Micah that he be involved with "my people." In his lamentation (1:8), not only his mourning but also his action for his people is revealed. He had gone stripped and naked and wailed like the ostrich and the jackal. According to the custom of ancient war, soldiers indiscriminately took men and women captives naked with them to their country. As a true prophet, Micah said he would also go stripped and naked with his people, so he first went to where his people were suffering and then shared in this suffering. From Micah we learn that the true prophet always stands on the side of the *minjung*.

The central issue for Micah was the suffering of "my people" who had been oppressed and dispossessed. Micah's attitude toward "my people" has provided us with an indication of the direction of *minjung* theology. The story of King Ahab who took Naboth's vineyard is similar to that of the plight of the *minjung*. Ahab is described as being the first man to have taken another's property by the abuse of power. However, there was no censure for this kind of behavior of kings during Micah's time. There was also no denunciation of the actions of the high officials who lived in the king's palace. Still, Micah spoke out against many of those who worked injustice. Micah singled out nobles, civil rulers (3:1-4), and false prophets (3:5-7) for special denunciation.

In the time of King Ahab, the fact that the king could not easily take the vineyard of a peasant indicates that this type of action was not common at the time. However, in the time of Micah this kind of activity was rampant, not only in the palace, but throughout society as well. And in Micah's denunciations of the thieves, there is no opportunity for repentance. Contrast this with Hosea 3:1, where God says to the prophet, "Go again, love a woman who is loved of a paramour and is an adulteress, even as the Lord loves the people of Israel, though they turn to other gods and love cakes of raisins." While in Hosea there is the possibility of repentance and forgiveness, in Micah this possibility is absent. The sin of idol worship spoken of in Hosea and the broad range of social evils and injustices in Micah were on different levels. To forgive the sin of the rulers which has jeopardized the survival of the *minjung* seems to be far more difficult than forgiving idolatry.

We can now establish that there are three characteristics of the prophesies of Micah which should be focused upon. One is that he always stood on the side of the oppressed people as their advocate. Another is that he prophesied not as a professional prophet like Amaziah, but as a commoner. The last is that he went to find "my people" in the places where they worked and lived, for the prophet Micah lived among the oppressed, the poverty-stricken, the laborers, and the sick in Jerusalem.

It is this focus that has formed the *minjung* theology in Korea. The three characteristics of Micah are the same that are beginning to take shape among theologians and leaders who are assuming the role of the voice of the *minjung* in Korea. Out of the oppression and suffering in Korea have emerged modern-day Micahs and Amoses—these people and their theology will be discussed in the next chapter.

The Rise of

Minjung Theology

It has already been noted that Korea is rapidly becoming a prosperous nation. Cities are growing, and new ones are constantly being built. The export business is flourishing, a fact clearly reflected in the steady rise in the nation's gross national product. However, this surge in the economy has not been without its cost. This newly achieved national wealth has redefined the line between the middle/upper classes and the *minjung*.

A clear result of this rapid industrial and technological growth in Korea has been the nearly complete transfer of wealth from the rural areas to the urban areas. Indeed, as Korea is thrusting itself into the world of high technology, many of those living in Korea's countryside have found that their traditional forms of labor are no longer in demand. No longer able to support themselves, they stream into the cities seeking the jobs that they dream will carry them into the ranks of the wealthy. However, this dream is seldom realized, and they end up instead with lives filled with exploitation.

The factory workers in Korea are a good example of this. The typical Korean factory worker is a sixteen-year-old girl. She works for nine hours a day, six days a week, for a meager twenty-six cents an hour. Her schedule of sleeping and working is alternated with those of other girls who work different shifts so that the factories never have to stop production. Often she must sleep on the floor of the factory so that, upon waking, she can go instantly back to work. Her diet is inadequate, and her working conditions are terrible. It is not uncommon for her to be forced to quit after a few years because of health problems. It is easy to see how the owners of the factories manage to reap huge profits because of this cheap labor. They put a great deal of pressure on the factory supervisors to meet huge quotas, which force the supervisors to bear down ever harder on the workers. This is just one example of the type of people who comprise the Korean *minjung*. Others include bus girls, bus drivers, taxi drivers, street cleaners, maids, prostitutes, street vendors. . . . The list goes on and on.

A method used by Lenski and Lenski to determine class distinctions and power can be used as a framework to better understand the position of these people in relation to those who hold power and wealth.[1] People are classified into various levels, depending on education, work, and income. Persons who involve themselves in social change are called "status inconsistent." To be status inconsistent means that a person relates to more than one socioeconomic level, for example, a woman physician with a high educational background and professional status who still faces sexual discrimination in terms of employment and pay. Status inconsistency leads to questioning the ranking order itself. "Status consistent," on the other hand, is the term used to refer to those who are secure in one socioeconomic level. People who are on the top of any system of social stratification, people who have been recently upwardly mobile in any system of stratification, and people who have been relatively stable in the system while parallel groups have been downwardly mobile all have a perceived vested interest in the status quo, whatever it is.[2] Because of their security, such people tend to be relatively uneasy with suggestions of drastic systemic change, reform, or revolution that would alter the distribution of goods and services. When they view ethical and moral questions, they tend to locate evil not in the social system, but at the individual level. Their discussions of morality and ethics will tend to focus on the individual and, if there is a problem, they will attempt to localize the problem within an individual or individuals.

Persons who are at the lower levels of the system of social stratification, persons who manifest status inconsistency, people who have been recently downwardly mobile, and people whose status has been static while others have been upwardly mobile — all of these groups tend to question the system of stratification. When they look at issues of ethics and morality, they are more ready to locate part of the evil as being within the system itself. When there is a problem, they are more willing to say that part of it is systemic and is not solely caused by individuals. These status inconsistent prophets are the ones who are willing to take the risks. They are the leaders who are willing to talk to the authorities. They are the ones teaching people—conscientizing them. And they are the ones holding up an alternative model of equality for all to see. For they, too, are *minjung.*

Thus, today, in the streets and on university campuses, ordinary people, intellectuals, laborers, and even poets have begun to proclaim the relevant messages of the Bible in the current economico-socio-political context of Korea. This movement has challenged the church in general. Some of those who have responded to the challenge have gone to prison willingly. We have been forced to formulate a theology of the *minjung* in order to furnish a biblical basis for the situation of the *minjung* who have been subjected to oppression and contempt. This theology can be truly called an indigenous, "grass-roots" theology, for it grew, and continues to grow, directly out of Christian experiences in the political struggle for justice. Moreover, *minjung* theology is Korean theology; it begins with the Korean *minjung,* their suffering and struggle. It is a theology of the oppressed in the Korean political situation, a theological response to the oppressors, and is for both the Korean church at large, as well as any who share in the struggle for liberation. This is what *minjung* theology is all about.[3]

The main objectives of *minjung* theologians are several. First, we wish to learn the truth about humanity, history, and God through the age-old experience of the *minjung.* We believe that truth becomes most apparent when it is looked at from the vantage point of the oppressed, and most comprehensive when it is searched for through the long history of the *minjung.* One's sense of the value of self becomes keener, the ability to discern good and evil becomes sharper, and the aspiration for a new and just society becomes firmer when one is oppressed and one's human rights are unjustly trampled upon.

We are also aware that God is revealed to us at this point of struggle in our lives, confirming our self-worth, justifying our discernment, encouraging our aspiration for a new tomorrow, and leading us to that future which is the destination of human history. This truth has been revealed to us little by little throughout the centuries as the *minjung* have struggled for their humanization. Therefore, the task of theologians is to examine the nature of the *minjung's* experiences, discover the hidden activities of God in them, and discern the significance of the discovery for our attempts to create a new and just society.

Finally, we want to formulate a theology which will help the *minjung's* struggle for a better tomorrow. This can be accomplished by clarifying the nature of the *minjung's* struggle and charting directions and guidelines for them to follow. Therefore, we believe that through the study of *minjung* theology we can learn not only about ourselves, but also about our adversaries, which is absolutely necessary if our work is to be effective. Furthermore, through the in-depth study of the *minjung's* experience in the Old Testament, we can discern the direction of human history which is important for the charting of our struggle.

What are our goals? First and foremost is equality. *Minjung* theology describes this equality as the unification of two elements: the renewal of human rights and the revolutionary change for justice in the social structure. In order to establish a society of equality, the *han*-ridden *minjung* must effect a drastic, systemic change in the existing order. In other words, the *minjung,* with the help of the insight derived from the Old Testament, must assume a new responsibility. This will strengthen their awareness of their bondage and offer them hope for liberation. Historically, such awareness often generates struggle and confrontation. Korea is already in the midst of some struggle but this new, conscientized struggle will have the proper direction, along with the lasting strength needed to reach its goals.

At the same time, it would be idealistic of us to assume that changes leading to true equality will come about easily. There will always be a stumbling block in our way—the pervasiveness of greed. This greed touches not only the oppressor but also the oppressed, and leads to the vicious cycle of imbalance and inequality. [4] We can see this so clearly in the history of Korea and in the story of Solomon which we examined in previous chapters. The cycle of the oppressed becoming the oppressor or the exploited taking on the role of the exploiter seems never-ending. But is it?

One possible answer to this question lies in the Korean concept of "dan" (斷). This is a Chinese word meaning "a cutting off" and represents the attempt to destroy the greed which is at the center of the oppressor-oppressed cycle. The cutting of the cycle of revenge would finally establish harmony in the political and social order. For the oppressors, it means that they should stop being greedy and oppressive. For the oppressed, it means that they should stop wishing to be like their masters and wanting to take revenge. Needless to say, we have discovered that neither of these transformations is easy to accomplish. Indeed, through cries and demonstrations the oppressed *minjung* have urged and demanded that the oppressors act in the spirit of *dan* and be fair. As demonstrations have escalated, however, the hearts of the rulers have hardened, and they have regressed further in the direction of evil. *Dan* is not easy for the oppressed either. Once liberation is achieved, it is difficult to resist the temptation to be like their masters and enjoy all the pleasure and comfort which they have been craving for so long. As a result, our hopes turn to the arrival of a Messiah to undertake this necessary exorcism. In fact, the messianic expectation is a common characteristic of all oppressed peoples. And the history of the Korean *minjung* is no exception, being full of such expectations. [5]

Crucial to active involvement in this exorcism is the seed of hope. Historically, seeds of hope have sprouted in various types of socio-economic soil, and the hopes have taken many forms. Generally, the oppressed have believed that the hoped for changes in the world will come about either by secular, political, and this-worldly struggle, or by the coming of a transcendent (metaphysical) power or person. The latter hope is most prevalent in Korea, though in varying shades, and takes the form of hope for a Messiah. Korea, being very "religious" at present, has diverse, and often bizarre, hopes in a transcendent messianism. Yet we cannot blatantly criticize these hopes without offering Old Testament-based correctives that express hope for a more just world in which peace prevails. Thus, it is to the Old Testament that we now turn to discern the seeds of messianism.

Messianic Hope
and Lifestyle

Messianism in Korea is a process in which the *minjung,* overcome by despair, look to the coming of the Messiah as their only hope. It is imperative that we carefully examine this emphasis, for in order to correctly shape and direct the future of Korea, we must first determine who this Messiah is. In doing this, we again look to the Old Testament.

The root of the word "messiah" means "anointed," an adjective that is not necessarily reserved for a divine or semidivine individual, and the primary connotation of "messiah" is not of a divine hero who is to come, but rather of a righteous and just liberator. When this is understood, we can more clearly understand the messianic expectation of the suffering people of Israel.

Anointing has historically fulfilled two different purposes. It has set apart that which is anointed and also has imparted the power to perform that for which the anointing is deemed necessary. At this point, it is well to say that, for the Hebrews, the "power" of the anointing oil was imparted by Yahweh. Thus, "the anointed" was in actuality "Yahweh's anointed." And what was the anointed to do? In short, he or she was to liberate and lead the people of Israel, establishing the victory of the justice of God over evil in history. There was perhaps another, more functional, reason for anointing: the urgent need to exorcise the evil desire for revenge which was common to all *minjung.*

Therefore, the Messiah for the Hebrews was not just a memory but a reality. Because of this, the equation of the kings and high priests with the Messiah created an irreconcilable contradiction. No king or high priest could possibly live up to the Hebraic ideal of the Messiah. Dissatisfaction with the kings and high priests grew, and this naturally led to a yearning, then a hope, and ultimately a belief that the coming "Great One" would bring liberation. The "day of Yahweh" was anxiously awaited. [1]

But what exactly was the "day of Yahweh"? From a study of the term, several possibilities come to light. The first suggestion is that, while the actual origin of the phrase "day of Yahweh" lies in obscurity, the term springs from Israel's own history and has roots in the records of God's intervention to liberate Israel from its enemies on numerous occasions, especially in battles.

A second suggestion is that the day of Yahweh always involves a special act of intervention by God in the affairs of humankind. There is no indication that the prophets thought in terms of only one day of Yahweh, but rather in terms of any act of God's intervention. In these acts of intervention there were special manifestations, not necessarily the same each time. Sometimes God would appear in person, in voice, or in action. Other times there would be heavenly signs in the sky or among the heavenly bodies. Still other times there would be disasters in the natural realm: hail, fire, earthquake, thunder, lightning, darkness, flood, locusts, famine, wind, whirlwind, cloud, pestilence, blindness, or plague. There would also be certain manifestations associated with warfare: panic, taking of spoil, captivity, battle, sword, noise, and blood. At any rate, whatever the sign, it would be God actively taking part in and controlling the affairs of humankind.

A third suggestion is that in the use of the actual term "day of Yahweh" by the prophets themselves there was always an element of God's wrath and judgment involved. This pronouncement of wrath and judgment was divided into two parts. First, the main emphasis of the prophets was God's punishment of God's own people for turning from God to the worship of idols, for social injustice, for violations of the moral laws, and for other sins. God's visitation upon Israel for its sins would be the coming of the day of Yahweh upon it. Second, God would pour God's wrath upon the nations of the world, sometimes individually and sometimes collectively. Their main crime was the mistreatment of God's people, the *minjung*. God's visitation upon the various nations would be the day of Yahweh upon the particular nations involved.

There is also the possibility that related to the day of Yahweh as it comes upon the nations is the theme of the restoration of Israel and Judah as one people again under the leadership of Yahweh. In the destruction of the nations and the restoration of God's people, God would be vindicated and glory would come to God's holy name. God would show the world that Israel's downfall was caused by its sins and not by the weakness of its God. Out of the fiery ordeal Israel would return to God cleansed and purified, a holy people. Some from among the nations would join with Israel in the worship of God.

Another suggestion is that there is little, if any, change in the concept of the day of Yahweh between the early and late prophets. The circumstances changed but the concept remained rather constant. Thus in the application of the term some differences can be pointed out. The main difference between the pre-exilic and the post-exilic prophets is found in the application of the term to Israel. The pre-exilic prophets, with the exception of Nahum and Habakkuk who limited their message to some foreign nations, were chiefly concerned with the day of Yahweh coming upon Israel, whereas the exilic and post-exilic prophets, with the exception of Malachi, were chiefly concerned with the day of Yahweh coming upon the nations in judgment. From this it is possible to conclude that the prophets considered the fall of Samaria and later that of Jerusalem as days of Yahweh upon God's people.

The final conclusion that can be drawn from this study of the concept of the day of Yahweh is that the prophets had extraordinary faith. From the days of Amos, when Israel and Judah were near the peak of prosperity in their status as two nations, until the fall of Jerusalem and beyond, the prophets could only predict and then watch the continuing decay and decline of their people until the national organization in the north and then in the south was dissolved. As Hosea expresses it, "The children of Israel shall abide many days without a king, and without a prince, and without a sacrifice, and without an image, and without an ephod, and without teraphim" (3:4). Thus were they brought down so that their cities would be, as it were, speaking "low out of the dust" (Isa. 29:4).

But as the prophets foresaw and then witnessed the horrors through which Israel passed, they proclaimed that it was Yahweh who was bringing these events to pass. It was the day of Yahweh. This conviction that the judgment proceeded from God also enabled the prophets to see beyond the day of destruction the day of the restoration of Israel by the Lord.

> I will destroy it from off the face of the earth ... I will command, and I will sift the house of Israel among all nations ... And I will bring about the restoration of my people Israel, and they shall build the waste cities, and inhabit them (Amos 9:8,9,14).

Thus the prophets showed that present and future disasters did not reveal any weakness in God. Instead, these cataclysms showed God's character and God's power. The prophets based their confidence on faith and hope rather than on sight, on the unchanging nature and power of God rather than on the passing gloomy panorama of contemporary history. They could see hope in disaster and a future bliss for those who were true to Yahweh. They believed that the messianic kingdom itself, once realized, should have the primary features of economic equality and social and political justice. In response to this *vision,* Israelites tried to develop a type of "messianic lifestyle." They consciously directed their lives by seeking to make them correspond to a messianic lifestyle within the changing economic situation. Thus, in order to promote economic equality, Israel chose to have the Sabbath, the Sabbatical Year, and the Year of Restoration. As we shall see, this promotion of economic equality is a very important aspect of *minjung* theology in Korea.

The Old Testament's view of human nature and life is very different on several levels from that of Korean society. In a number of places the Old Testament clearly and emphatically criticizes the fundamental social condition of Korean culture: the privileged people are in opposition to the *minjung.* The Book of Deuteronomy (15:12-14) commands that "you are to release a fellow Israelite slave after he has served you for six years, and do not send him away empty-handed." Deuteronomy 15:15 then presents the rationale behind this command: "Remember that you were slaves in Egypt and the Lord your God set you free." Since all of the Hebrews were, in one way or another, originally slaves, they could be called *minjung;* they were treated cruelly and were led into forced labor by other nations. However, they were liberated, and settled in Canaan, the supposed promised land of milk and honey.

While in Canaan, the Hebrews created for themselves an extremely great disparity between the rich and the poor, and the rich made the poor their slaves. This kind of behavior reveals the destructive attitudes that exist against the liberating acts of God, for the rich were behaving like their former cruel oppressors, the Egyptians, toward their fellow Hebrew citizens. Those who were enslaved in Egypt were still slaves in Canaan. The Hebrews were only relocated, not granted humanity as the subjects of history. Their liberation amounted to nothing because of the economic greed and self-centeredness of the rich.

Thus, the Sabbatical (or Seventh) Year was instituted to teach the Hebrews economic equality. The message behind this was clear: "Don't exploit each other, for you are all human beings!"

The concepts of the Seventh Year and the Year of Jubilee need to be related to the Korean government and the situation in our society. If in Korea the distance between the rich and the poor is of such magnitude, where does the Korean government stand in relation to these two groups? For example, the rich have already built extremely luxurious houses, and others are planning even larger mansions. We must ask: What is a mammoth house for? Should the people not be as concerned with pouring their time and money into building a more just society for the *minjung?* We call upon the Korean government to stop constructing huge buildings and put down the hammer, to establish a moratorium and think about the direction into which it is heading. No matter how splendid the buildings, they simply become arenas for personalities, powers, and forces to work against justice and equality.

The Seventh Year and the Year of Jubilee are extensions and/or enforcements of the Sabbath. According to Exodus 34:21a the Sabbath is a day to stop work and take a rest. The Sabbath was established in order to set us free from being working slaves. In Exodus 20:8, God commands us to move from the state of "taking a negative rest" to that of taking a positive attitude: "Observe the Sabbath and keep it holy!" In Deuteronomy 5:12, the concept is slightly changed and expanded: "Observe the Sabbath and keep it holy, as I, the Lord your god, have commanded you." But how do we "remember," "observe," and "keep it holy"? The answer is extremely explicit and clear: "No one is to work!"

If we are to keep the Sabbath, why then do we neglect to keep the Seventh Year and the Jubilee Year, which are so closely related to the Sabbath? The *minjung* need a sabbath rest; they need to have their burden relieved in order that oppression and toil might not characterize all the days of their lives. The motivation behind the regulations of the Seventh Year and the commandment to keep the Sabbath is the same. The basic commandment was originally not a demand, but a privilege to be free from demands. It is a commandment as well as a gift. The Sabbath and the Seventh Year are gifts of free time.

Leviticus 25:1-7 explicitly explains this gift: "The seventh year is to be a year of complete rest for the land." This is parallel to the "Sabbath, a day of rest for man." The commandment of the Sabbath rejects avaricious pursuits of wealth and exploitation. Likewise, the commandment of the Seventh Year deplores the blatant misuse of the land. The freedom to rest on the Sabbath means that all of Israel's time originates in such freedom and liberation. Likewise, rest for the land in the Seventh Year is an indication that all the land of Israel has been given as Yahweh's gift of liberation to the people. If this fact is overlooked, a land of liberation will become a land of slavery, and consequently it will result in the slavery of the *minjung*. Furthermore, according to Exodus 23:10-11, the commandment of the Seventh Year originally meant that all things growing in the fields should be given to the poor and the animals rather than being sold for profit. In these passages, the theological implications of the commandments are not emphasized, and as a result more emphasis is placed on the human meaning of the Seventh Year. From Exodus we see that in the Seventh Year, the land, vineyard, and olive grove should lie fallow and nothing that grows on the land should be harvested; the poor may eat what grows there, and the wild animals can have what is left.

This kind of policy was implemented to minimize, to a certain degree, the envious feelings and expectations of the *minjung,* the basic purpose of this being to promote a lifestyle of mutual equality. Thereafter, the Seventh Year was linked with the next stage of setting the slaves free and discharging people from their debts, these being more positive aspects of these policies. Deuteronomy says, "Everyone who has lent money to a fellow Israelite is to cancel the debt; he must not try to collect the money" (15:2). Here, the Seventh Year is the Year of Release, and a deep concern for the welfare of every individual in the community is expressed. It is not merely a principle of living according to one's own ability and power, but is rather the principle that everyone's need should be met in accordance with his or her want. The law of the Seventh Year was given to the Israelites in order to protect the poor and unfortunate. Thus, the law was different from the ancient secular laws, which were based on the principles of social class, power, and wealth. In other words, according to the principle of the Year of Release, the purpose of an economic system is to protect the weak, the poor, and the helpless — the *minjung*.

The basis of Israelite theology was the events of the Exodus. The Year of Release was created in order to set the Israelites free from the bondage of being in slavery in an alien land: "You were slaves in Egypt and the Lord your God has set you free" (Deut. 15:15). On this basis, the Hebrews responded to the command of God to cancel the debts (vv. 1-11) and set the slaves free (vv. 12-18). The Year of Release was an attempt to allow the *minjung* to regain their humanity as the subjects of history. Thus, Israel came to proclaim the Year of Release for the Hebrews. The proclamation was an action for the sake of God, and the result was to give liberation and freedom to the *minjung* and to the slaves. The creditor declares release for the debtor, and the slaves are set free, allowed to go and have a just and fair chance in life.

The positive acts of cancellation of debts and release of slaves are deeply related to Jesus' criteria for the judgment: "I was hungry and you fed me, thirsty and you gave me drink; I was a stranger and you received me into your home" (Mt. 25:35). Here we see that Jesus identified himself with the poor and the weak: "Whenever you did this for one of the least of these brothers [and sisters] of mine, you did it to me!" (Mt. 25:40).

The commandment of the Seventh Year is also directly related to human blessedness. Deuteronomy 15:5a says that "if you obey God and carefully observe everything that I command you today, the Lord will bless you," and in verses 7-12, the notion is colored with a psychological ethos:

> If in any of the towns in the land that the Lord your God is giving
> you there is a fellow Israelite in need, then do not be selfish and
> refuse to help him . . . Do not refuse to lend him something, just
> because the year when debts are cancelled is near. Do not let such
> an evil thought enter your mind. If you refuse to make the loan, he
> will cry out to the Lord against you, and you will be held guilty . . .
> Give to him freely and unselfishly . . . If a fellow-Israelite, man or
> woman, sells himself to you as a slave, you are to release him after
> he has served you for six years. When the seventh year comes, you
> must let him go free, . . . and the Lord will bless you in everything
> you do.

If the Korean government and the church keep the Sabbath, then
they should be compelled to keep the commandment of the Seventh
Year which insists on economic equality and freedom for all, as this
was also commanded forcefully by God (Deut. 15:7-18). In addition,
just as the people of Israel failed to keep the commandments and
subsequently lost their nation, the future of Korea will not be exempt
from God's judgment if it fails to keep the commandments.

In later periods, the custom of the Seventh Year was extended to
include another type of regulation called the Jubilee Year or the Year
of Restoration. This was the year after the Seventh Year had passed
through seven times, so it was the fiftieth year (7 x 7 = 49, plus the
next year). The priestly code (e.g., Lev. 25:8-24) made a connection
between the Year of Restoration and the message of freedom, empha-
sizing that the Year of Restoration was the great time of releasing
debtors, setting the slaves free, and giving a rest to the land. It was a
year of amnesty, because all of the slaves, the land, and the debtors
were discharged in that particular year. It was the Jubilee Year for the
minjung, because it was possible to rejoice after a long, long journey of
restriction as slaves and debtors. Thus, the Year of Restoration was the
minjung's social institution for the prohibition of endless expansion of
land possession, the restoration of lost houses, the release from heavy
debts, the liberation of hopeless slaves, and the formation of a truly
free and equal society. Let us look more closely at the details of the
contents of the Year of Restoration from the viewpoint of the priestly
code in Leviticus.

1. The land: Land was not to be sold on a permanent basis,
because people did not own it; it belonged only to God, and people

were like foreigners who were allowed to make use of it (25:23). However, in the case of the poor, the selling of land was permitted. If an Israelite became poor and was forced to sell land, his closest relative was to buy it. A man who had no relative to buy his land and had to sell it to someone else could later, if he became prosperous, buy it back for himself. In that case, he was to pay the first man who bought it a sum that would make up for the years remaining until the next Year of Restoration. In that year all land would be returned to its original owner. In this sense, the commandment of the Year of Restoration did not simply mean rest from labor, but also prevented persons from possessing vast expanses of land, which is the fundamental basis of wealth in an agricultural society. Thus, the Year of Restoration was a revelation of God's principle of impartial sharing of land and helped satisfy the human need for possession.

2. Housing: Houses in unwalled villages were treated similarly to the fields. If they had to be sold, the original owner had the right to buy them back, and they were to be returned in the Year of Restoration. But if a man sold a house in a walled city, he had the right to buy it back during the first full year after the date of sale. If he did not buy it back within that year, he lost the right of repurchase, and the houses became the permanent property of the purchaser. Levites had the right to buy back at any time their property in the cities assigned to them — though it was to be returned in the Year of Restoration — because the houses which the Levites owned in their cities were their permanent property. Here, we find the same principle of protecting the poor *minjung,* the rural villagers, and the Levite *minjung.*

3. Money and Food: Israelites were responsible to provide for poor fellow Israelites, loaning them money without interest, so that they could continue to live nearby. In Leviticus 25:35-39, the notion that "he can continue to live near you" is repeated three times. Verse 38 says that "God brought you out of Egypt in order to give you the land of Canaan and to be your God." It is clear that if the Israelites could not live near each other, both the events of the Exodus and the giving of the land of Canaan would be invalid. This has important implications. Many people these days are trying to attain a high standard of living and think that "high living" is a blessing from God. However, there are great dangers in being wrapped up in this endless struggle

for pleasure. What the Old Testament emphasizes here is not to live well, but to live near one another on an equal level.

From the economic perspective, it may seem unjust to be forced to lend money or food without any profit or interest. However, what the Old Testament refers to here is not an economic principle. It is a decision that comes from God's behavior towards the poor and the rich. In God's opinion, the rich should lend money and food to the poor and should not demand any interest on these loans. We must face the problem of whether we will believe and obey God or just follow economic principles. In all of our actions, we should witness to the essence and meaning of being the body of Jesus in society.

4. Slaves: Because the people of Israel had been liberated from Egypt, they were not to be sold into slavery or become so poor that they had to sell themselves to fellow Israelites and thereby become enslaved *minjung,* as they were in Egypt. Rather, poor Israelites were to stay with fellow Israelites as hired hands and serve them until the next Year of Restoration, when they were to be liberated. It was a principle of releasing slaves. In the Year of Restoration, all persons were able to return to their clan and could regain ownership of their land.

All of the Israelites considered restrictions as temporary, as that which passed by after a little while. The Israelites, the people of God, observed the Sabbath, the Seventh Year, and the Year of Restoration as their institutions. These were firmly connected with their hope for freedom and justice. They were granted such institutions of liberation in order to be a liberated people, rather than the slaves of labor, poverty, and corrupt institutions. They were not to become *minjung.* Thus, the Israelites' hope for freedom continued to stay alive, even in difficult times, such as those preceding and following their Babylonian exile.

According to Isaiah 61:1-2, the messenger of joy has come "to bring good news to the poor, to heal the broken-hearted, to announce release to captives and freedom to those who are in prison." In Joel 3:1, an eschatological reference, Yahweh also appears for the restoration of freedom and equality. In the lamentations of the Psalms, we find that the *minjung* request justice directly from Yahweh, because God had promised to hear their voices (Ps. 12:6, 22:25). There are no

differences between slaves and free persons; we are all one in un....
with Jesus Christ (Gal. 3: 28). Are there differences between the rich
elite and the multitude of *minjung* in our society?

How do we give a sound answer to the above question? The
answer may not demand a logical form of explanation but takes its
form in two ways. If we engage in acts of faith for the *minjung,* we
shall be a liberated people. If we do not, then we shall be a nomadic
people who are the captives of contemporary Babylons. We should
practice acts of faith for the *minjung* and stimulate God's people to
open their palms to their poor sisters and brothers. The essential
questions for us become, What is the real role of the Koreans in society? Do we take seriously God's commandment to eliminate the difference between the poor and the rich in building a just society? Can
we practice the abandonment of possessions every seventh year ?

The practice of self-abandonment should begin with us, and we
must continue until equality between the poor and rich is accomplished. No matter how rich we are, of what use is the wealth if it moves us
into the hands of faithless people? If we do not attempt to realize the
will of God, then we have already changed into some institution which
cannot be called the Christian community.

It might be argued that the Year of Restoration or the Seventh
Year as observed by the ancient Hebrews has nothing to do with us in
the modern world. However, we can see that the regulations of the
Seventh Year have consistently undergone revision. The commandment
is for an institution in which freedom and equality are given by God to
the people, and it has always been reinterpreted concretely in the
changing social structures. However, the will of God—to give freedom
and equality to the poor and the oppressed, the *minjung* of our world—
still continues.

If we come to understand these concepts, we will realize that if
we stand only in our self-centeredness, we cannot bring to fruition the
democratic movement that will provide us with freedom and equality.
In order to confront all elements which hinder equality and freedom,
we must expand our service beyond Korea. We must demonstrate to
the world this Old Testament idea through our practice of it. There
should be faithful celebration of the Year of Restoration in which we
share our own property directly with the poor. We should be the voices

of contemporary prophets proclaiming God's will for the institution of the Seventh Year and the Year of Restoration today.

8.

Conclusion

The *minjung* are subjects of history. Whether they are consciously aware and involved or passively idle, the *minjung* are the focus of God's concern here and now. They are a permanent historical reality which has generally been determined in relation to the power which has been in command. Yet at the same time, they are the protagonists in the historical drama. Not fully aware of the power which they possess in their powerlessness, the *minjung* transcend the power structure.

As we have already discussed in the previous chapters, the *minjung* should be understood within the framework of the relation of the ruler to the ruled, the ruled being the *minjung*. We have defined the oppressed as being those who have their political, social and cultural rights infringed upon. Furthermore, we have regarded the Exodus as the *minjung's* movement for liberation. In our opinion, it would be correct to say that *minjung* designates those who are the "objects of liberation."

Kim Chi-Ha has spoken of the *minjung* from another point of view. [1] He asserts that, according to Genesis 1:28-30, the *minjung* are the embodiment of the universal human being. Therefore, *minjung* refers to those who reform human history, to those who, with the right of subduing and ruling the earth, fulfill the objectives of God's creation. [2] It is this latter goal which we should pursue further.

In my earlier work on *minjung* theology, [3] I noted that the essence of the Old Testament can be regarded as being *minjung* theology, and that the Old Testament is the history of belief in the *minjung's* liberation movement and the creation of humanity. In contrast, we generally regard the *minjung* as persons under the domination of a ruling system. But the Old Testament has described the *minjung* subjectively, calling them the crown of God's creation. Therefore, in a positive sense, we can define *minjung* in the context of their relationship with God as human beings.

In Genesis 1:28-30 the *minjung* appear in their original form (prototype) as the objects of God's blessing. God blessed them and said to them, "Be fruitful and multiply, and fill the earth and subdue it; and have dominion over all other living things." Nevertheless, as we have already seen, there is also a reverse form (antitype) of the *minjung*. For example, because the Hebrews were prolific and strong, the Pharaoh tried to stifle their privilege to be fruitful and multiply by slaughtering the newborn Hebrew males. Supervisors were placed over them, and they suffered under exceptionally heavy burdens in all of their work. These were the hardships of the Hebrews under slavery. For these reasons, the God-given call of the *minjung* to fill the earth and have dominion over it could not be realized. Moreover, they had fallen into the position of being mere slaves ruled by Egypt. The distance between their situation in Egypt and the divine providence of God's creation was great.

God's blessing was a bold and clear affirmation of the intention of the divine sovereignty. The intention was that, whatever the situation, God's will could not be overcome. God's sovereignty would be asserted despite the captivity of the *minjung.* God's assertion of sovereignty in Genesis 1 is contrasted to a reality filled with poverty, defeat, and despair. However, the historical reality can and should be changed to the reality of God's peace and joy. The five God-given privileges in the Genesis text affirm God's original intent for the *minjung.* God completed the creation of human beings by entrusting them with the duty of maintaining the order of God's world, a world which God desires to be fertile and plentiful.

If we compare the historical situation of the period of the exile in Babylon with that described in Genesis 1:28 (since the creation account was finally written during that exile), Genesis 1 becomes a refutation of helplessness and oppression. The call and blessing of Genesis promises an end to barrenness and a lack of heirs, as well as to being crowded out, subservient, and dominated.[4] This proclamation of Genesis is strikingly appropriate to a people in exilic conditions who are homeless, rootless, and alienated from their land and traditions.[5] It is an affirmation that their God is still in charge and that their destiny therefore still offers blessing and dominion. The word of hope is an amazing challenge to a hopeless historical situation.

In today's world, the God-given rights of human beings necessarily take on new and broader meanings. The special relationship of human beings with the world and with other creatures needs to be emphasized. One of the purposes of creation is for human beings to dominate the earth and the animals, but it is not right for human beings to dominate their fellow human beings. It is not part of human destiny that any human lord should dominate the people. This domination may be inevitable in certain situations, but it is not intrinsic to human life. The argument that some people were born to be slaves is not consistent with the Old Testament understanding of human beings as creatures of God.

Finally, all people have the right to bodily sustenance. This has special meaning if we remember that food is required to prolong life and that the body, as part of the human being, is the temple of God. Human beings have the responsibility to preserve that precious temple.

Some theologies emphasize only the salvation of the human soul, thus restricting God to the work of forgiving sins and leading persons to heaven. However, this emphasis misinterprets the totality of God's intention, which is related to the concrete reality of human beings. As a result, many people today are not interested in the dignity of humans, which is an essential part of the Old Testament message. Genesis 1:27 speaks of the dignity of human beings, and this theme is found throughout the Bible. The phrase about the creation of human beings, "Let us make man [human beings] in our own image and likeness" indicates that the human being is more than spirit and thus this statement is not in accord with a purely spiritually-oriented theology. This phrase focuses on what it means to be human and emphasizes the dignity of all humans as God's creatures. This relation to God is an important concept in our understanding of human beings.

What exactly does the phrase "God's image and likeness" mean? It is a proclamation about the value of *all* human beings, not just a few select individuals. The fact that God made the decision to create human beings in God's own image indicates their special position as the head of creation and as the subjects of history. It also implies a unique relationship between God and humanity. The created has been endowed with the ability to communicate with the creator God.

If the meaning of God's image is found not in the unique characteristics of human beings, but rather in becoming human, then all differences between human beings, between religions, and between Christians and non-Christians disappear. One must instead come to an understanding that to bear the image of God means to come from God; that is to say, one is "a part" of God. God is like a sculptor, as it were, who carves several stone statues out of a very large rock. Thus, each human, although different from all others, bears the image of God.

The fact that human beings are created in the image of God, underscores the great value of human beings. The basis of human dignity lies in the fact that the human being is God's creation. Dignity is contained within all human beings, in each individual member of the human race.

However, there is a very important problem in accurately expressing human dignity. Human dignity comes from outside the sphere of the human race. The Bible comments not only on human values, but also on the meaning of being human. The human race is being created through certain events which occur in the relationship between God and human beings and in which the meaning of being human is grounded.

The term *minjung* preserves the full dignity of the human being. The *minjung* as humans are destined to become the subjects of history. They must define their own existence and generate new acts and dramas in their human history. They must transcend the present socio-economico-political determination of history.

We should recognize the fact that the *minjung* are not yet fully the subjects of history. However, their role as subjects is being realized through their struggles against oppression, exploitation, and repressive social structures. In these struggles, the *minjung* have risen up to be subjects of their own destiny, refusing to be condemned to being objects of manipulation and suppression. The *minjung* have their own stories to tell, which are in contrast to the stories or the dominant ideologies of the rulers. When we say that the *minjung* are the subjects of history, we are not exalting them in political terms. Rather, we are simply affirming as authentic their identification of themselves as the crown of God's creation, as those who should be masters of their history which is told in their socio-economico-political biography.[6] Thus, human history should be of the *minjung,* by the *minjung,* and for the *minjung,* for they are the subjects of history.

Much work is yet to be done. The problems of the *minjung* should not be considered to be solely their concern. On the contrary, all parts of society must take an active interest in their plight. This includes the Korean churches.

Presently, there is real tension in the Korean churches between two types of Christians. One group is still holding on to the fundamentalistic belief of Christian life, continuing the "Egyptian Captivity" of the years between 1920 and 1945. While these Christians are not interested in the social and political affairs of life, they are enthusiastically evangelistic. They fervently believe in prayers and hold daylight prayer meetings daily. Afterwards, they fast and listen to high pressure preaching. Their prayers are filled with personal petitions and requests for the conversion of relatives, intercessory prayer for others being almost nonexistent among them. Another important aspect of these churches is the charismatic movement which has spread considerably amongst them.

It appears that the main reason these Christians still cling to their beliefs is that many of them are all too aware of the risk involved in a struggle for freedom. Persecutions under the Japanese, under the communists in the North, and under the present totalitarian regime have forced them to be realistic about church and state. However, one of the major criticisms of these churches is directed at their naive understanding of the Christian truth, for the principle of separation of church and state must also include the right to disobey state when it conflicts with Christian beliefs. But they have failed to fully understand the meaning of this principle, neglecting their duty to prophesy and follow the exemplary life of Jesus Christ.

The other group of Christians, on the other hand, have not only emphasized the evangelistic aspect of spiritual life but are also aware of the concept of missio dei. [7] Out of some eight million Christians in 200 denominations (61 registered with the government) more than three million Christians belong to the six major denominations that are members of the Korean National Council of Churches (KNCC). These Christians hope and pray that the Korean churches will get together to serve as witnesses to the great mission work of God as they manifest the commitment of Christians in Korea to the cause of the further expansion of God's kingdom. This is a real manifestation of the spirit of ecumenism. In order to achieve this goal of expanding God's kingdom, the following issues have been considered as important by the KNCC since the 1970s:

1. First of all, the domination of church relations by Western power centers must be overcome and churches in the so-called mission field must realize their authentic subjecthood.

2. Maturity and autonomy (self-determination) should be fully respected in relations and cooperation on the international level. This means that international justice as well as Christian solidarity are integral to the ecumenical relationship.

3. Ecumenical relations and cooperation of churches on the international level should be set in the context of secular ecumenical relations with the *minjung* in different nations. This should also be firmly based upon theological and historical foundations, which means that interchurch relations should include *interminjung* relations for justice and peace.

Korean churches have actively participated in Korean society through their pronouncements and actions. The areas of participation have been social mission and human rights. The social mission includes rural mission, industrial mission, urban mission, and mission work among students and intellectuals. In particular, the human rights movement of the Korean churches has forced strong solidarity with the democratic forces in the Korean society at large. The missionaries from the Presbyterian Church in the USA, the United Church of Australia, the United Methodist Church in the USA, the Presbyterian Church in Canada, German churches, and so on, have all become coworkers with the Korean church leaders and with all Christian people as partners in Jesus Christ, affirming that we, together with Korean churches, believe in the same God, the one church of Jesus Christ, and one mission to carry out.

Meanwhile, it is shocking that the same Christianity that advocates the democratization of political power in Korea today has become a threat in the form of the absolutization of authority carried out on the basis of an anti-communist ideology. It is a fact that the political power that is waging a crusade against the communist dictatorship in North Korea has itself become dictatorial, both in form and content. It has taken on a demonic character, depriving people of their freedom, integrity, and human rights. It uses people as ideological tools to achieve its ambition for absolute power. Within such a political system of physical and spiritual regimentation, a mere plea for the democratization of power is regarded as insurrectionary. It becomes treason to call for the liberation of the *minjung* from the oppressive power of a repressive government. But the theology of *minjung* that emerged from the outcries of the suffering people in Korea is precisely concerned with liberation, not only from physical slavery or suffering, but also from exploitation for political and economic purposes.

Thus, the Korean churches must take the initiative in this movement towards liberation. We must impress the concepts of the Sabbath, the Seventh Year, and the Jubilee Year upon the Korean government. We must call upon the government to pay heed to the disparity between the rich and the poor, to focus upon the issues of justice and equality, and to work to build a society fit for all its people and not just the upper crust. Korea has advanced rapidly; progress made in industrialization and urbanization is astounding, However, even in this time of work and progress, a time for rest must be found for those upon whose backs and with whose labor the successes of Korea have been built. The *minjung* must find rest; they must have a Sabbath so that their every waking moment need not be filled with oppression and toil.

Not only the Korean government but also the churches must keep the Sabbath and strive toward the ideals of the commandment of the Seventh Year and the Year of Restoration with their insistence upon economic equality and freedom for all. Korean pastors continue to be overly concerned about the size of their congregation, the size of their church building, and the needs of individual salvation. This means that they neglect the call to create a just and equitable society for all of God's people.

The people of Korea have a great desire to be "whole" and the churches have been extremely slow in their awareness of this fact. The churches cling to a religious messianism and tend to force their despair into an eschatological framework, preventing them from dealing effectively with present realities. Therefore, other types of messianism develop outside of the churches: for instance, faith in technology, in economic growth, or in purely political solutions. The churches must wake up to their individualism and blindness and help to shape a new society. It is the society itself, its excesses and policies, which force the *minjung* into their *han*-ridden existence. Instead of pouring their time and money into new buildings, the churches must redirect those resources toward building a more just society for the *minjung*.

This is the challenge before the churches in Korea today. They must discontinue avoiding the reality of oppression, an escapism that only helps to perpetuate the injustices as they are. Instead, they must act. Moreover, they must continue to develop an indigenous theology and continue to discern certain fundamental values such as the *minjung* and the Korean churches as subjects and not objects of history.

As the Korean churches, under the guidance of the Holy Spirit, venture forward into the future, these are some of the directions they must take:

1. The Korean churches should emphasize *human* (body and soul) liberation and the qualitative enhancement of the whole life of the Korean society—a development that is necessary to bring about true liberation. The following two tasks should be involved in the churches' mission.

2. On the political level, the Korean churches should continue to work for the realization of a democratic society and national unification in which the participation of the *minjung* is guaranteed.

3. On the economic level, the Korean churches should try to form a self-reliant economy centering on the basic needs of the *minjung* and their welfare.

However, even as other parts of society have a part to play in the light of the *minjung,* it is imperative that the *minjung* themselves realize that they are oppressed and come to terms with the injustices under which they live. This process of conscientization leads them to assume responsibility and work toward their liberation. Koreans as a people are invited to act as partners of God. Historically, an awareness on the part of the *minjung* as to their condition and its ramifications has often preceded God's intervention. Even if this should take the form of struggle, confrontation, or revolution, we cannot evade our responsibility as partners of God. We are called to a position of modern-day Micahs—advocating the human rights and dignity of the oppressed, identifying with them, and searching for them in the places where they live and work. We must act in faith, and in so doing we work not only to free the *minjung*, but also to liberate ourselves.

Notes

INTRODUCTION

1.   Suh Kwang -sun David, "Korean Theological Development in the 1970s," in *Minjung Theology* , e.d. the Commission on Theological Concerns of the Christian Conference of Asia (CTC-CCA), (Maryknoll, N.Y.: Orbis Books, 1983), p.41.

2.   Ibid., p. 42.

3.   See Walter Brueggemann, *Prophetic Imagination* (Philadelphia: Fortress Press, 1973), pp. 33ff.

4.   Suh, "Korean Theological Development," p. 42.

CHAPTER ONE: AN INTRODUCTION TO THE *MINJUNG*

1.   Kim Yong-bock, "Messiah and Minjung: Discerning Messianic Politics over against Political Messianism," in *Minjung Theology,* ed. CTC-CCA (Maryknoll, N.Y.: Orbis Books, 1983), p. 183.

2.   Han Wan-sang, "Minjung, the Suffering Servant and Hope," (Unpublished lecture delivered at James Memorial Chapel, Union Theological Seminary, New York, April 13, 1982), quoted to me by Hyun Young-hak.

3.   Suh Nam-dong, "Historical References for a Theology of Minjung," in *Minjung Theology,* p. 157.

4.   Moon Tong-hwan Stephen, "Korean Minjung Theology: An Introduction," (Unpublished paper delivered January 1982), p. 2.

CHAPTER TWO: THE HEBREWS AND THE EXODUS

1.   There is no agreement among the scholars who take the view that the Exodus took place in the thirteenth century B.C. as to who the actual Pharaoh was when Moses liberated his people from Egypt. Some believe that Ramses II was the pharaoh of the oppression as well as that of the

Exodus, and there are those who date the Exodus as being during the time of Maniptah, the son of Ramses II. The problem lies in the Old Testament reference to the death of the Pharaoh from whom Moses had fled. If we assume that it was Sethi I who initiated the oppression, then we would have some difficulty in accounting for Moses' stay of forty years in Egypt and an equal stay in Midian before returning to liberate his people near the end of Ramses II's reign. Of course, it has been suggested with some plausibility that the period of forty years is often taken as a round figure to describe a generation, and that the actual figure would be much lower, say twenty-five years. Even though we are not able to solve the chronological problem satisfactorily, the reign of Ramses II seems to be at the time of Moses' challenge to Pharaoh.

2. M. C. Astour, "Habiru, Hapiru," in The *Interpreter's Dictionary of the Bible*, supplementary volume (Nashville: Abingdom, 1976), pp. 382-85.

3. Marvin L. Chaney, "Ancient Palestinian Peasant Movements and the Formation of Premonarchic Israel," forthcoming in *Biblical Archaelogist*.

4. For a more detailed study on *han*, see Suh Nam-dong, "Towards a Theology of *Han*," in *Minjung Theology*, ed. CTC-CCA (Maryknoll, N.Y.: Orbis Books, 1983), pp. 55ff.

5. Rachel Young-jin Moon, "A Study of the Change in Status of the Korean Woman from Ancient Times through the Yi Period" (Dissertation, Emory University, Atlanta, 1982), pp. 4-16.

6. Kim Yong-bock, "Korean Christianity as a Messianic Movement of the People," in *Minjung Theology*, p. 81.

7. Ibid.

8. Ibid.

9. Ibid.

10. Ibid., p. 82.

11. Ibid., p. 83.

12. Choo Chai-yong, "A Brief Sketch of Korean Christian History from the Minjung Perspective," in *Minjung Theology*, p. 75.

13. Kim Yong-bock, "Messiah and Minjung," in *Minjung Theology*, p. 188.

14. Ibid.

15. Choo Chai-yong, "Brief Sketch," p. 76.

16. Ibid.

17. Kim Yong-bock, "Korean Christianity," p. 86.

18. Ibid., p. 88.

19. Ibid., p. 95.

20. W. L. Swallen, Preface to *Sunday School Lessons on the Book of Exodus* (Seoul: Religious Tract Society, 1907).

CHAPTER THREE: THE HEBREWS IN PRE-MONARCHICAL CANAAN

1. Cf. J. A. Callaway, "New Evidence on the Conquest of Ai," *Journal of Biblical Literature* 87 (1968): 312ff.

2. From the Conquest Model we may conclude that the destruction of Canaanite cities occurred in the late thirteenth or early twelfth centuries. Hebrews under the leadership of Joshua might not be the only destroyers

of the ancient cities as the Old Testament evidence claims; some archaeological data show that it might be possible that the Egyptians and Canaanites brought destruction to some or all of the cities. If the Israelites carried out the destruction, they did so not as a twelve-tribe unit , but as the proto-Israelite group that later became the components of the biblical Israel.

3. A most helpful resource containing both sides of the argument is the *Journal for the Study of the Old Testament,* no. 7 (May 1978).

4. George Mendenhall, "The Hebrew Conquest of Palestine," *Biblical Archaeologist* 25 (September 1962): 71.

5. Walter Brueggemann defines the alternative consciousness as " a movement of protest which is situated among the disinherited and which articulates its theological vision in terms of a God who decisively intrudes, even against seemingly impenetrable institutions and orderings" ("Trajectories in Old Testament Literature and the Sociology of Ancient Israel," *Journal of Biblical Literature* 98 [1980]: 162).

6. Norman K. Gottwald, *The Tribes of Yahweh* (Maryknoll, N.Y.: Orbis Books, 1979), p. 214.

7. Ibid.

8. Brueggemann, "Trajectories," p. 162.

9. Han Woo-keun, *The History of Korea* (Seoul: Eul-Yoo Publishing Company, 1984), p. 507.

10. Ibid., p. 508.

CHAPTER FOUR: SOLOMON, THE CREATOR OF THE VICTIMS OF SOCIAL INJUSTICES

1. John Bright, *A History of Israel,* 2nd ed. (Philadelphia: Westminster Press, 1972), pp. 212-15.

2. Ibid., pp. 211-12.

3. Robert Wilson, *Prophecy and Society in Ancient Israel* (Philadelphia: Fortress Press, 1980), pp. 302-3.

4. ✓ Walter Brueggemann, *Prophetic Imagination* (Philadelphia: Fortress Press, 1973), pp. 33ff.

5. Bright, *Israel,* p. 214.

6. Ibid., p. 207.

7. Ibid., p. 217.

8. Gerhard Lenski, *Power and Privilege: A Theory of Social Stratification* (New York: McGraw-Hill, 1966), p. 286.

9. Ibid.

10. Ibid.

11. Ibid., pp. 294-95.

CHAPTER FIVE: PROPHETS AND THE HELPLESS, POOR, AND OPPRESSED

1. Hans Walter Wolff, *Joel and Amos: A Commentary on the Books of Joel and Amos*, Hermeneia Series (Philadelphia: Fortress Press, 1977), p. 90.
2. Ibid.
3. See Walter Brueggemann, *Prophetic Imagination* (Philadelphia: Fortress Press, 1973), p. 32.
4. Wolff, *Joel and Amos*, p. 205.
5. James Mays, *Amos* (London: SCM Press, 1969), p. 142.
6. Brueggemann, "Trajectories in Old Testament Literature and the Sociology of Ancient Israel," *Journal of Biblical Literature* 98 (1980): 172.
7. Ibid.

CHAPTER SIX: THE RISE OF *MINJUNG* THEO-LOGY

1. Cf. Jean and Gerhard Lenski, *Human Societies: An Introduction to Macrosociology* (New York: McGraw-Hill, 1982), pp. 211ff.
2. Marvin L. Chaney, "Ancient Palestinian Peasant Movements and the Formation of Premonarchic Israel," forthcoming in *Biblical Archaeologist*.
3. Moon Hee-suk Cyris, "An Old Testament Understanding of Minjung," in *Minjung Theology*, ed. CTC-CCA (Maryknoll, N.Y.: Orbis Books, 1983), pp. 123ff.
4. Choi Je-u, who founded the Donghak Movement in 1860, explicitly warned against greed as a cause of oppression. Although he was disillusioned, he was a religiously sensitive person. He was sometimes called Choi Messiah. His teaching may be summarized in three phrases: love of people, particularly of weak ones; care of one's body; and purging of greed. He saw greed as the root of all evil. See Moon Tong-hwan Stephen, "Korean Minjung Theology: An Introduction" (Unpublished paper delivered January 1982), p. 5.
5. Ibid., pp. 5-6.

CHAPTER SEVEN: MESSIANIC HOPE AND LIFE-STYLE

1. There has been a dispute among many scholars whether or not the term "messiah" is used in connection with the "day of Yahweh." But these terms are definitely related to the *minjung's* hope in God's approaching intervention in history to judge the oppressors. God's judgment would be for the benefit of the *minjung*, and sufferings would come to an end. See John M.P. Smith, "The Day of the Lord," *The American Journal of Theology* 5 (July 1901): 509; and G. von Rad, "The Origin of the Concept of the Day of Yahweh," *Journal of Semitic Studies* 4 (April 1959): 109.

CHAPTER EIGHT: CONCLUSION

1. Kim Chi Ha is a poet. He participated in the student revolt that toppled Syngman Rhee in 1960. In 1975 he was nominated for the Nobel Prize in both Peace and Literature.
2. Suh Nam-dong, "Historical References for a Theology of Minjung," in *Minjung Theology*, ed. CTC-CCA (Maryknoll, N.Y.: Orbis Books, 1983), p. 155.
3. Moon Hee-suk Cyris, "An Old Testament Understanding of Minjung," in *Minjung Theology*, pp. 123ff.
4. Walter Brueggemann, *The Vitality of the Old Testament Traditions* (Atlanta: John Knox Press, 1969), p. 128.
5. Ibid.
6. Kim Yong-bock, "Messiah and Minjung," in *Minjung Theology*, p. 186.
7. *Missio dei* is a Latin term which means " the mission of God".